Farmer's Diary

Charlie Allan

Illustrations by
Turnbull

Ardo Publishing Company
Methlick, Aberdeenshire AB41 0HR

I am grateful to the Glasgow *Herald* for permission
to reproduce these articles, which first appeared
in print in that newspaper.

C.A.

Published by Ardo Publishing Company, Buchan
Printed by Famedram Publishers Ltd, Aberdeenshire

Foreword

DESPITE the fact that our store is still overflowing with unsold copies of Volume One of this farmer's diary, it has been decided to try a second volume and a third is even planned. Having made enough off Volume One to buy the Jag, the only hope of paying the fuel bills necessary to keep her ghosting along the road seems to be to try further volumes.

You may well think that this, being as it is, no more than a collection of articles reproduced more or less as they appeared in the Herald, would be the very easiest type of book to put together. And you may well be right but it was my inability to get all those articles together, to assemble all Jim Turnbull's cartoons, to figure out which cartoons should go with which article, and to figure out which article went with which date, that prevented this appearing a year ago.

Indeed publication would never have happened had the author's breadwinner, wife, and stern critic not taken on the job. If sales are better than with the Volume One I will always be grateful. And even if we lose money on the deal I will admire, as I have so often in our thirty-three years together, her tireless pursuit of order. My preference for words and her preference for deeds are the secrets of our success as a couple. Mind you, there is no room for doubting who would eat best if we were rent asunder. Deeds pay better than words.

I am again indebted to Jim Turnbull for the permission to reproduce his excellent cartoons which, as well as illuminating the text, are helpful to those who haven't the time, patience or expertise for reading.

My thanks are due to Stroma, Beverly, and Maris at *The Herald* library for help with various missing links, to the Mses Names, Williams and Macintosh™ at Famedram for their help with spelling and punctuation. Where eccentricities remain they are mostly at my insistence. The Breadwinner and Eleanor Stewart did the desk-top publishing without complaint.

I thank them all but most of all, I thank you for reading, (even) this far.

*This volume is dedicated to those families who were
farming at the end of the war and who now have been
forced off the land. I hope they won't think that the jolly tone
of this book means I am careless or that I haven't been
close enough to see what giving up would be like.*

THERE IS no need to go over the chronology of disaster that spanned the years of his birth to the starting point of this volume as that was done well (if selectively) in Volume One. But a brief reminder of the author's history as a farmer might be helpful.

In 1973 he took over from his late father John R. Allan, and proudly assumed the roll of fifth generation and bunnet laird of Little Ardo farm. He was able to acquire the two (1958 and 1960) Fordson Majors, two hundred and fifty acres, a fine view over the river Ythan to Bennachie, and an overdraft.

The steading had been falling down when his grandfather, the late Dr Maitland Mackie, bought the place from the lairds of Aberdeen in 1923, so a building programme was started. That and an ambition to have more cattle than Little Ardo could possibly support saw the herd built up from nothing to seven hundred and the overdraft from a hundred to a thousand pounds an acre.

Despite the obvious soundness of this business plan a strat-

5

egy of retrenchment was worked out with both sets of bankers.

By 1989 the overdraft was again down to about a hundred pounds and acre, the tractors were both from the 1970s, the old steading was still falling down and the herd was down to four pure Simmental cows.

A brilliant if crazy scheme to have a herd of forty Jerseys as hill cows and transplant beef calves into them was tried with a success which will unfold in the course of this volume. But as Volume Two starts, the key to success seems to lie in improving the cereals. If only the local Grain Barons could be persuaded to part with their secrets.

The Farmer's social life revolves round the friends with whom he meets on Sunday night at the Salmon Inn to exchange ideas and slake the thirsts developed in a week of toil. Those include the Grain Barons, Mossie and the Red Rooster, Crookie the Potato King, Gowkie, the sma' hudder with whom the Farmer used to carouse as a boy, Big Hamish who has a dairy and a digger the wheels from which cost more than all the Little Ardo machinery put together, neighbours Hillie and The Mains, and Potions the local chemist who would so have liked to be a farmer that he comes to Little Ardo to play at it. If there were more workers like Potions the wage bills of the industry would be easily handled.

The Farmer's helpmate is the Breadwinner. While the farm struggles she works in the toon for the price of a fat stot a week. She has two daughters who are good hardworking girls and have the sense to stay away and get on with winning their own bread. The family is completed by the Farmer's two sons, the Wasting Assets. They are delightful people who, despite not being as young as they were, still haven't made the connection between earning money and spending it; they have a talent for one but no inclination towards the other. If it doesn't interfere with their social life the Wasting Assets may be available to act as gates and to do other undemanding work about the farm.

There are still only three grandchildren but the threat is still there.

Struggling against the stones

I WILL try to explain to you about the peasant's regard for his land as it hits me. Love is part of it of course but it is too weak to describe the relationship between myself and this place. 'Love' is too cosy... too self-satisfied. 'Awe' is more like it.

I am in awe of the fertility that my forebears have found in this once-blasted heath. I am in awe of the river Ythan which never stopped even in the height of the drought and which is a motorway for the salmon and sea trout. I am in awe of the thousands of geese that overfly us, just out of range, every day in winter.

But I'm not so keen on the stones which seem to form the majority of this hill. I couldn't even say that I love them.

The struggle against nature which is my heritage has always been fought with stones as one of the adversaries. In clearing the fields we built the steadings and the house with some of them, and dry stone dykes with more. And Little Ardo has many thousands of tonnes of stones cowped or in beautifully built consumption dykes... monuments to the toil that has left us enough loam for the plough.

I was minded to talk about stones today by two things.

The first is the news that a hard-pressed farmer in Cumbria has been selling his stone dykes. The economics look attractive. He is reported as getting ten pounds a metre for the stone and replacing it with a wire fence for one pound and fifty pence.

Now, there are approximately eight miles of dykes at Little Ardo so if I could tap into this market I reckon I could raise £120,000. Then there's the mile of dykes my father carted away in an effort to make our fields big enough for modern machinery and the half mile that I did away with for the same reason. No doubt the three hundred yards we buried will come up in time providing a continuing source of revenue. And of course we must have an acre of stone gatherings.

But that's all speculation. I hope and believe that Little Ardo will always be a stock farm, and there is very little shelter on either side of a barbed wire fence.

The other thing that put me in mind of stones this week was the fact that I have been given the job of sorting up a prehistoric stone circle.

During the war, when my father was fighting the Hun and my mother was lending her skill as a schoolteacher to the war effort, I stayed with my grandparents at North Ythsie of Tarves and it was then that I first came across the stone circle.

It was on the neighbouring farm of South Ythsie and I used oftentimes to go there in summer and play "Tack ye" among the stones with my pals or sit on the close grazed grass, my back on a standing stone, stringing the gowans.

I had no idea then that there were similar stone circles all over the North East or that my one was three and a half thousand years old.

They were set up by the first farmers, the people who took the first bold steps toward taming the wilderness. No one knows for sure what they were for but they were a great work. I have seen calculations which suggest that more than a hundred men would have been required to erect some of the bigger stones. In those days there was no Big Hamish to come with his digger and no ten pounds an hour with which to pay him. Everything had to be done by hand.

It is possible that the standing stones were an early calendar… when the sun at midday cast the shadow of the big stone to the foot of the little stone with the crack in it it may have been time to sow the crop. But what is sure is that the stone circles had a religious function and a social one too. The stone circles were meeting places for feasting and other indulgence.

I can vouch for that last as, when I was a student and when midsummer came, some of the hotter bloods used to repair to the stone circle at Daviot for what was no doubt a pale celebration of the old revelries.

So you can see that I am very happy to have acquired a certain responsibility for the stone circle at South Ythsie.

A cousin of mine, Maitland Mackie, has done absolutely the right thing by buying (back) the farm which was once our grandfather's home farm. And he has also bought South Ythsie and has brought my stone circle into the family.

I visited it the other day. After forty-six years it is still there and still magical. The six great stones are still standing in their circle though they are only about half as big as they were. When last I visited them they towered above my head. Now the smallest one doesn't come much above my knee.

Of course that's largely because of what has happened to me in those forty-six years, but not solely. Generations of ploughmen have found my circle a suitable tip for the yearly crop of stone-gatherings so that the grass on which I used to sit is completely covered... and so are part of the standing stones.

But the circle is there and I've got the job of clearing the foreign bodies, putting up the fence, laying the path, erecting the sign and arranging for the goat to keep the grass trimmed for future generations of small boys.

It is a job much to my liking. I hope I haven't confused you by saying that I couldn't love stones. I was talking about the stones which lie on the ground or skulk beneath it to break the power harrow. Standing stones are different. They are a hotline to my ancestors.

Trouble began on Christmas day

THERE'S SOMETHING to be said for working over the holiday period. It lasts so long these days that if you really do take it as a holiday, and if you accept all the food and drink that's going, you end up bloated and tired.

Much better, I think, to work over the holiday and then you end up just as tired, but at least you recover more quickly.

With the exception of my two Christmases under the equatorial sun in Kenya, I've always chosen to be on duty. For one thing it gives you a grand excuse for turning down any invitations you don't want, and it also gives you a good excuse to leave the celebrations in the smaller hours of the morning rather than waiting for the serious damage which is done later on.

I had that old Bing Crosby film in mind in 1975 – the first year in which I told the lads to go off on Christmas Eve and not to come back until the fourth. Bing had got fed up of being in show-business where he had to put on an extra show at every holiday. He would get away from it all by becoming a farmer.

He can't have known many farmers, for any could have told him he was to be bitterly disappointed.

The rest of the film showed our hero struggling with his livestock, and his machinery until it came to Christmas day itself when he found he hadn't the stomach for his turkey on the grounds that he had known it personally.

Of course Bing's main trouble was that he couldn't do the job – he couldn't even work a graip let alone the sophisticated mechanical aids I would have at my disposal. It would be fine to get the two men's holidays out of the way, and, if all went well, I would never have to work more than four hours a day.

But all did not go well. For that you need everything where it should be, and to know where

everything should be. Feed for every beast should be handy, and they should all be well bedded.

On Christmas morning my troubles started. All the animals' water had frozen except for that in the slatted court. I decided that the 30 which were still outside could drink snow. The other 200 had to be watered by hand. That morning, and for the next two, I had to take out buckets of hot water to thaw the handiest taps and then bucket feed the lot.

The only good thing was that it it is nice to be appreciated and they fairly appreciated the water I brought them – and the funny thing is, the less I brought the more they appreciated what I did bring.

I was reminded of the boy who, in the days of tied cattle and before the advent of the drinking bowl, was always so quick at watering the bullocks. Eventually he foolishly confided his secret – if you put a little bit of sharn in each pail the water went a lot further.

The shop opened the day after Boxing Day and I was able to get a hose, but that was the day of the thaw and the floods which soaked all the bedding.

Apart from the water

Christmas day was the worst. None of the inside beasts had been bedded. Straw had to be taken from the barn, but the tractors had been parked so that I couldn't get at the International with it's nice heated cab unless someone gave me a tow to start the 5000 which was a slow starter on frosty mornings. So I was reduced to the old Power Major – and a roll bar is little comfort in a blizzard.

There was no bruising done for the 150 barley beefers. I didn't mind doing some bruising though I shouldn't have had to – but no-one had told me that to get one of the augers to work you had to push a Phillips screw driver inside the switch and then give a dunt on the wall. That meant the bruising had to be done onto the floor, bagged, and manhandled round to the beasts.

My friend the Methlick baker sorted that one for me when he was first footing, but I still shudder when I think of the risks we took in mixing 480 volts and 70 proof.

I shouldn't have been surprised that looking after 400 cattle and 10 hangovers would be a full-time job, especially in arctic conditions. But with proper preparations it has always been tolerable since.

But in that bad year the crescendo of my rage peaked on New Year's Day. As the only one working, it of course fell on me to pull all the revellers out of the snowdrifts they landed in. I understood that. But my fury knew no bounds when, as I was freezing along in the cabless Major to feed the outside beasts, I found the gate blocked by a car abandoned by one of the blades who had left me in such an appalling state of unreadiness.

Perhaps the one good thing about the old Major was its rear loader. And with only a moment's hesitation I picked the offending car up and deposited it on the dyke.

I won't be complaining this year though. I have no staff now so, like Bing Crosby, I'll have no-one to blame but myself.

Aiming to maximise the take

Rise up guid wife
And shak yer fedders.
Dinna think that we are beggars.
We're only bairnies
Come to play.
Rise up
And gie's wir Hogmanay.

SO WE sang when we were young. Round the houses we went, me and my pal Albert, on Hogmanay. We sang out- side doors we'd be feart to knock at any other day of the year. And no one who had experienced it could forget

13

the warmth of the welcome. The well stoked fire, the unfamiliar smell of whisky already beginning to turn sour on the breath, the sweeties, the dumpling, the shortbread, and the eager enquiry as to what we would sing next.

We only had one encore for two reasons. *Mormond Braes* was the only other song Albert could sing and I had figured that the way to maximise the take was to spend as little time as possible in each of as many houses as possible.

We got a wonderful reception for, in truth, the tradition of the bairns seeking their Hogmanay was dying fast in the North East and we had the field more or less to ourselves.

I remember especially the last time we went out. We took a couple of shopping bags for the loot, though we tactfully left those outside the houses in case, in displaying our wealth, we inhibit people's generosity. We had spiced up our act too by setting *Rise up Guid Wife* to the tune *The First Noel* and set off early to get in as many houses as possible.

We got all we could eat, all we could carry, and a considerable sum of money. Not only that, but we were plied with enough drink to have foun-

dered lesser men. It was perhaps a warning of appetites to come that I arrived home very late on January the first warm but none the worse of the drink.

That is how I remember it and I discovered the other day that my memory is not as bad as it might have been and that my capacity for self-deceiving exaggeration is not as great as many would have you believe.

I came across the following entry in my father's diary for 1950. *January first – Charles and Albert went seeking their Hogmanay with a neepy lantern. Got much cake, fruit, port wine and lemonade and 4 shillings and a penny each in cash. Charles came back at half past midnight.* We were eleven years old and had been all over the countryside, and no one had given a moment's thought to our safety.

Those diaries give other clues as to how life has changed on this farm. Hogmanay was the time for presents and Christmas just didn't rate at all. The twenty-fifth of December was a working day like any other. The farmer might take his family to a relative for a Christmas dinner but the six men worked on as normal.

The ten years of my father's diaries have the following entries for Christmas day: *1949 – A day of great lassitude; 1950 – Threshing barley; 1951 – Threshing barley. 107 qrs in the day; 1952 – Bright clear day; 1953 – John Salmon says graders at some English centres collect £200 a day in bribes. It seems impossible and yet it could be.* From 1947 to 1956 the only mention of Christmas was *1947 – Christmas Day dawned bright and clear.*

But Hogmanay was a quite different story. *1947 – Rattray (second tractorman) dashing about Methlick like a steer; 1949 – A great day of peace and quiet, but the evening, it would appear, was not so quiet. Even Bob Gray (the orraman), they say, was unco newsy. Bill Taylor (foreman), driving one of the hotel cars, coupit it on the Doctor's Brae. It took fire but everybody got clear; 1950 – The baillie got home in time for the milking. Said if he'd gone to bed he would never have risen again. Skelmie (neighbouring farmer) reportedly going round the village with his fists clenched above his head and roaring like a polar bear.*

And what of 1990 at Little Ardo?

Well the staff (that's me) still had to work on both holidays, but we managed to celebrate both. The little church was full for the watchnight service and we followed that with too much food and drink on Christmas day.

Hogmanay was planned as another musical prelude. Instead of boggling at the box as has become usual we would have a family evening singing the old farming songs. The theory was that a more active evening would cut down on the drink and let us away to bed just after midnight feeling that we had done justice to 1990 and given a sufficient welcome to 1991.

We had the *Muckin o' Geordie's Byre, Bogie's Bonnie Belle* about the farm servant who lost his job because he had helped the farmer's daughter to lose her honour, *Drumdelgie* which catalogued the horseman's day from five in the morning to eight at night. We wallowed in the nostalgia of *The Buchan Plooman* who would "*ca yer horse or sort yer nowt or big a ruck o' strae*" and still be "*as happy as a lark frae dawn tae dark*". And we sung the truer ballads which celebrated the hey-days of the fairm toons by complaining of them. The ploughman's great strength was his freedom to leave and that he usually did after six months or a year.

> *Oh fare ye weel*
> *Drumdelgie.*
> *I bid ye a' adieu*
> *I leave ye as I found ye.*
> *A maist unceevil crew.*

The evening was good fun. It was almost as uplifting as the watchnight service and it did keep the tele off.

The only bit that didn't work out was the going off to bed soon after midnight.

Serious attack by pigeons

I MIGHT have known everything would go wrong when we didn't get our first foot until five o'clock on New Year's day. He was reasonably tall, quite dark and very handsome, but just too late.

It's such a shame too as I started the year with such high hopes and good intentions. I would do everything timeously (making the entries in the drugs and herd books, for example, and tattooing and dishorning at once rather than when there was time). I would get on with all those jobs that had been hanging about (putting the other half of the loose box roof back on, claiming the grant for the replacement of the lead pipes in the house and sorting my late father's papers out).

The troubles started on New Year's day when the pigeons made their first serious attack of the winter. With the snow, frost and wind their attention has again turned to the oil-seed rape.

We've 40 per cent more rape than last year and it is looking plucky rather than well. It was a bit later sown this year and got a much more hostile reception from the weather. Mossie, who knows absolutely everything about combinable crops, says the worse crops are looking at this time the better they'll do at harvest. "All show no dough" he keeps saying.

If he's right I'll have a bumper harvest this year. But my crops consultant is really alarmed. He says the rape is so thin that I mustn't let a single pigeon land on my 66 acres.

It is great to be a consultant. You advise, retire to the bar, and return in three weeks to shake your head at everything that hasn't been done. It is all right for him to say "keep the doos off", it's me has to do it.

And so it was that I spent five hours on January the first, standing in the high winds and sleet, daring the doos to come anywhere near my rape. And so it was that by night time I was hardly able to swallow the ex-

tra dram that I had surely earned.

After a sleepless night in mortal fear of having to cough again I got the doctor to open his surgery on the morning of the second. He prescribed antibiotics and bed… he's as bad as the crops consultant. He only sees part of the problem.

The Cruelty will be after me if I don't feed and bed my cattle and if I take the doctor's advice, the doos will make off with my harvest.

Shivering, headaches and hacking coughs are most of what I remember of the third but Willie the Hunter says he appeared and promised to take care of the pigeons. I know I was very ill that day for I poured a dram of ten year old Macallan back into the bottle.

On the fourth I awakened a little refreshed and with a sense that I was through the worst. At eight o'clock the excellent Armstrong arrived from the Buchan Machinery Ring. He would take over the feeding and bedding, and bruise up enough barley to keep me going for a week.

Now, the bruising system was designed by another consultant and is far too clever to work. It consists of five augers, an elevator and a conveyer with droppers.

We were hardly started when everything from the elevator back jammed solid. It was enough to stop our 75 horsepower tractor.

To a background of indignant bellowing from the hungry cattle we proceeded to unjam the bruiser, two augers and the elevator. We knew that the problem was in the elevator because it had started on the three previous occasions once we had that unjammed.

As the wind howled and the sleet turned to snow, I was the one who sat on the cold cement floor and fished away with the soup ladle getting always a little more barley off the pack. Being ill I gave the Armstrong the job of going up the ladder to work away at the top with our two foot stilson.

I will have to be at death's door before I make that mistake again. "Mind your head", came the roar. I threw myself backwards and as my knees came up to where my head had been the nine pound stilson hit me full on that fleshy muscle above the knee. The Armstrong, who wasn't as alarmed as me but was impressed, said the stilson hit me so squarely that it actually bounced.

Nothing was broken but even that good luck wouldn't persuade me to work on. I sent for the millwright.

And what a lesson that was. Though you can save a lot by DIY there are some things better left to the professional, however dear he may seem.

It took him two minutes to find the two inspection hatches which would have let us free the machinery in five minutes. It took him another minute to see that the trouble was barley building up on the sprockets which over-tightened the chain, and another two minutes to clean them. The wright then spent an hour repairing all the unofficial inspection holes we had made and the cattle got fed.

That night as I tried the Macallan again I reflected on a sad start to the year. I had had an outbreak of pneumonia among the calves, foul of the foot among the cows and some reveller had left the gate open and let the donkeys escape. There I was with a knee which made the wearing of long trousers impossible. On top of that the room was spinning, my fever was coming back and I was the main man again the next day.

The fever turned out only to be dehydration. I'm now on the mend and I promise to be cheerier next week... even if I have to cheat.

Arrival of new boarders

THE POPULATION of the farm has risen from 114 to 314, not counting the wood-pigeons. For on Wednesday we took delivery of 200 ten week old pigs. If all goes to plan, they'll all be off to market in ten weeks time and I'll be a richer man.

God knows I can use it. We've had a visit from our management accountant and he tells me that my beef enterprise only made three hundred pounds of a contribution to the farm's overheads last year... and don't forget my labour is just one of those overheads. In layman's language the cattle made a whacking loss so I felt I had to find a new way to earn my daily bread.

But why pigs?

Are pigs not the most cyclical farm product of all? Do not they swing from boom to bust with alarming regularity? And did I not have pigs once before and lose money on them like I didn't think was possible? And do they not make a terrible smell?

A wise man, who was also old once told me... indeed like so many old men who say wise things he was forever telling me... that the pigs only smell when they are losing money.

My previous flirtation with pig keeping was in the seventies when a cousin (who had seen the flaws in the system) was wanting out of Rodenight pigs and saw me as the means whereby he could get out profitably. He sold me forty sows in pig, forty arcs, and enough feeders to do the job.

We set up the arcs in three separate fields and filled one field at a time as they pigged. Soon we had all the arcs full and each field teamed with delightful pink sausages charging around in happy packs in the summer sunshine. When they approached weaning weights we took the piglets inside and sold them at sixty pounds liveweight. We were able to wean 10.3 pigs per sow, the price was right, the first batch

had paid up the investment and even provided seventy gilts to expand the enterprise. I looked forward to a steady stream of income and there wasn't a hint of smell about the farm.

The gilts pigged in a snow storm and started me on a nightmare from which my banker has more or less recovered but my head never quite can.

The gilts did everything wrong including pigging two and three to the arc, no doubt in an effort to keep warm. That led to cannibalism, followed by dysentery and pneumonia. I know of no more depressing sight in farming than that made by my vet at that time. He was wandering about in a sea of pink, picking up the odd piggy and squirting stuff into it's

mouth. He wasn't able to tell me what was wrong, which pigs he had treated nor what to do next.

We eventually cleared the trouble up with in-feed antibiotics, but not before four of the nine live births per litter had been lost.

And it turned out that those which had been lost were the best payers. The others had been damaged by their illness. Their appetites were quite undiminished but their ability to turn food into flesh seemed to have disappeared altogether. They were eating a thousand pounds a week and getting no bigger, or so it seemed.

The money ran out. The North Eastern Farmer's rep (who was the only man who was making any money off the deal) offered to give me feed to finish this lot and see me through to another farrowing in return for my entire year's harvest.

Thank goodness I resisted that temptation. I weaned them all and raised enough from the sale of the sows to finish all but the worst stragglers. The last dozen or so would be with me yet if I hadn't decided to let the knackery have them.

Now those pigs did leave an awful smell about the place.

With a history like that, why on earth would I be going back into pigs now?

Well, for a start, I'm not going into the breeding end of the business this time. There is, as yet, no proof that I'm no good at fattening pigs. And the risk is very low this time because I am to rear those pigs for Grampian Country Pork. They provide the capital and take the risk.

My two hundred grunters and squealers don't belong to me. They are just boarders. The company provides the feed. I provide the straw, the shed, the water and the stockmanship. If I keep the death rate below one per cent and achieve a conversion rate of 2.8 per cent the company will pay me £4 a head after ten weeks... and I'll get to keep all the muck.

If I manage to kill them all that will be the company's loss, though I don't suppose they would ask me to keep another batch in such a case.

Of course Mossie is absolutely disgusted with me for being so timid as to let the company finance the deal. "T' hell wi' lettin them get a' the profit", he says. But then he and I have entirely different farming experience. I see it as the company taking all the losses.

Mossie is taking in 500 extra piggies to fatten himself and says I am going to miss out. Apparently the price has slumped from 140 pence to 92 pence. This, according to Mossie, is bound to be reversed. As long as I stay in I am bound to catch the rise... but not if I let Grampian take the risk. Too bad.

But there is one part of the deal upon which Mossie and I do see eye to eye. I am allowed one per cent of deaths and we both agree that with his fine new barbecue made out of the converted rotaspreader, we should be able to guarantee that the company do 'lose' one per cent.

Pigeon battle hots up

MY LITTLE bit of Buchan has taken on something of the air of the Somme in the 1914-18 war as we farmers do battle against the millions of pigeons which are pillaging our rape. Last year's oil seeds grossed £430 an acre – so it's a battle we are determined to win.

It's not going to be easy though. The mild winter last year and so far this year have meant that the wood pigeons have bred virtually all the year round and there are literally millions within a short flight of this farm.

For that we have to thank Haddo House Estate for growing their woods at Haddo and at Gight. From their estates there, the Earls of Aberdeen have for centuries sent forth a plague of vermin to plague the poor tenants. The rabbits were once a terrible scourge, though they are less so since myxomatosis. And the roe deer seem to prefer peasants' trees to the Laird's.

Haddo House also keeps some of the finest rookeries in the North-East. Rooks know how to strip a field of potatoes, and this year they are adding to their notoriety by pecking out the wheat by the root, supposedly in their search for Tory worms. I fear those leather jacket larvae are one kind of Tory still abundant in Scotland.

Then there are the pheasants. I have to admit that, even in the days when we were all tenants and weren't supposed to shoot the laird's game, we were always quite glad to see the odd pheasant.

But this plague of cushet doos is something else. I think it's partly because of the success of oil-seed rape here that they have increased in numbers so dramatically – the tender shoots give an abundant and nutritious fodder for the birds all through the winter.

And with the absence of any snow cover to speak of lately, there just hasn't been a time when nature thinned the pigeons down.

We farmers are doing our best though. From first light the air is full of thousands of beautiful blue rape harvesters, and each day I and a hundred anxious neighbours hurry to get the beasts done in time to be ready for the first raid.

There's no telling where they'll strike. Sometimes they fill the sky for 10 minutes at a time – all swarming off for a juicy bite far to the north of Little Ardo. But sometimes they decide mine is on the menu, and then they are really hard to stop. Last year we had a 24-acre field stripped in January of every leaf.

I've three fields totalling 66 acres this year and though I filled them up with abandoned cars to make them look busy, and though I have a hide in each, I find that one of me isn't nearly enough. When I blast off at the first flight they simply head off and attack one of the other fields.

Now, I have a pal in the village who is a renowned mercenary in pigeon wars. He has often shot a hundred in a flight, so I've engaged Willie to fight for me this year. I have to report though that the move hasn't been entirely successful. You see Willie is a hunter and I am a farmer, and we work badly as a team. The hunter seeks to kill pigeons, whereas all the farmer wants to do is protect his crops.

Willie is in charge of operations, gauging the wind to set the hide right, and setting out the decoys with their heads to the wind. Then we await the invader. What he wants is a sure shot. He reckons to kill 95 birds with 100 cartridges, so the hunter wants them nice and close.

He would happily watch a thousand pigeons grazing their way across the field towards him in anticipation of a clear shot. But that hardly suits me – it's my rape they're grazing after all. So as soon as I see a pigeon that looks likely to land, I'm blasting off at it in the hope that it will fly off to one of my neighbour's fields. The Hunter shakes his head and wonders at the stupidity of the Farmer.

I could of course give up the pretence of hunting and join those of my neighbours who've gone over entirely to psychological warfare. Despite the evidence that they are quite useless after a short time, the land is ablaze once again with gas guns which tear the winter silence apart every few minutes whether there are pigeons about or not.

Some sceptics do even say that the gas guns are used by the cushets to locate suitable crops. The theory is that if the farmer employs a banger, he must reckon the crop is ready for eating and he must also have decided not to do any real shooting.

I can't say I believe that exactly, but I don't like the gas guns. It is a bit better now that most people have photosensitive switches, which at least turn the damned things off at night, though we do have one neighbour who's got the latest even noisier howitzer which blasts away at the moon.

I don't yet know who it is, but when I find out I'll need his phone number – and there's no knowing when I might call. After all, even on the Somme they had the occasional lull.

Consumer friendly piggies

MY TWO hundred little piggies are fattening before my eyes. At least they should be for they are putting away about half a tonne of feed a day. They seem happy enough too but I don't suppose they know how lucky they are. I'm sure they don't realise they are 'animal welfare pigs' or 'consumer friendly pigs'.

Instead of being born in wire cages and reared in slatted boxes these have been born in little huts in fields that grow grass in summer and mud in winter. There they suckle with the north wind on their backs for up to four weeks before coming into a sawdust bedded shed to start the serious business of converting cereals into pork while the mums squelch across the mud to the next field to visit the boar.

After three weeks on sawdust the young pigs go into courts bedded with straw where they are expected to turn pellets into pork at the rate of 2.8

pounds of feed to 1.0 pounds of meat. They have a hundred and ninety-nine pals to play with, big bales to bore about in, tyres and a ball to bite, and all they can eat available at all times. Having known the discomfort of a Scottish winter outside, they are in an ideal position to relish their cosy beds.

They are high health pigs too; in theory they should never be ill. Indeed the only thing my piggies have to worry about is reaching a weight of 65 kilos. Then they have to go to market.

A lot of thought has gone into devising this pig-friendly rearing system. It's not because the farmers were looking for a happier pig. With the exception of the sow stalls, which fewer and fewer people are willing to defend, most of us suspect that most of the factory system of rearing pigs suits the pig quite well. No, the pressure comes from the consumers and their agents are the supermarkets.

Several of the big chains have come to Grampian Country Pork and offered them a contract to rear pork to a specification. That's as common as muck, of course, but these specifications are not simply the traditional ones dealing with fattiness and taste, for example. The modern contract also specifies living conditions for the pig. Those include being born outside, being reared on straw and having a minimum amount of room per pig in the fattening house.

This is a very interesting trend but, in my opinion, we should not be at all surprised about it. The supermarkets want to be able to say to their customers that they are offering pork that has been raised with the minimum of what the consumers regard as cruelty to the animals.

You see most food in Britain is no longer required to satisfy nutritional needs... it does feed us of course, but the satisfaction of hunger is hardly in it. Indeed the less nutritious food is, the better.

That point was brought home to me when I was in Africa. And it was most clearly demonstrated by the television advertising. There the theme is how fat your wife and children can become if they eat the product. The families who are depicted enjoying the wonders of "Mchuzi Mix" would never get in a commercial for food here unless it was one of those before and after jobs. They are too well fed to advertise food here.

What our advertisers want is thin people to show how much we can eat and still look like famine relief posters. If

27

food were still about feeding people we would be able to stop at cabbage broze and a suppy cream.

No, food production is best seen as part of the entertainment industry. We are not trying to feed people we are trying to give them a good time.

So we should not be surprised that people are starting to worry about how their food is produced. If they eat to feel good, we should not be surprised if they want to feel good about how their food is produced.

So mine are consumer-friendly pigs.

I don't know if the pigs are any better off under the system but it certainly looks a pleasanter outfit than the one my grandfather, Maitland Mackie, used to keep at North Ythsie. Whenever there were visitors, which was every day, we went on the tour of the piggery. The old man took his working boots off when he was thirty-four and when he took us round the pigs it was in a pair of rubber galloshes pulled over his shoes.

The piggery had a dark dusty cobwebby central pass off which were doors which slid back to reveal unlit hell-holes carpeted with two lots of porkers which were fed dust from a central pass. Putting the light on sent them surging to the narrow door which led to the outrun where they were expected to dung.

Having suppressed their shock and made admiring noises the visitors were then taken to the office (the table beside the weighing machine). There, in the statistical department (the south wall) there was recorded each pen's food intake and weight gain... for the whole lot was weighed every week. The old man used to tell me that a conversion rate of 3 was possible though the best he ever managed was 3.3.

I heard a rumble of thunder the other day which I thought might have been the old man trying to get in touch. He built the Little Ardo piggery and would undoubtedly be delighted to see it full again. The shortage of feed during the war stopped the pigs and for some reason the piggery has never been restocked till now.

Still, the old man put up a flexible building. I have only had to spend £300 on feeders to get it back into production after fifty years. And curiously that is exactly what the old man spent when he started from scratch in 1936. £300 was the original cost of the whole shed.

February 11, 1991

Piggies clean up the dung

I HAVE a friend who farms in the land of milk and money, in Kansas City Missouri to be precise. There, the business for which he has earned a reputation stretching back to his native Scotland, is pedigree Simmental cattle. What takes most of the time though, is his cattle feedlot where he fattens whatever is looking cheap in the market. But the only thing which makes money year in year out is what he calls his 'hoggs'. When he was a boy Gordon Phillip would have called them 'pigs', and I was most intrigued at the reason why the pigs do so consistently well. The secret lies in the feed which costs absolutely nothing.

You see Gordon runs his hoggs along with his feeding cattle. The steers are fed nothing but maize and a mineral supplement, while the pigs aren't fed at all. They are just too short in the leg to reach up to the hoppers.

Despite the apparently parsimonious rations the pigs do well and the secret lies in the extraordinary high fibre qualities of the maize. That ensures that the sweetcorn passes through the steers so quickly that there are plenty of nutrients left for the pig in the bovine droppings.

The trick is to have just enough hoggs to use up all the cattle waste without leaving the piggies hungry. I think maybe Gordon was cutting that a bit fine when I visited him in '82 because there was considerable competition for the food available.

As you know cattle tend to defecate when they stand up so any steer showing signs of rising was immediately surrounded by eager little piggies. Gordon even told me that clever hoggs would steal up behind a steer and give him a sharp nip to make him get up. Mind you, I think my friend may have been letting the imagination for which we in the north east are famous run away

29

with him on that occasion.

Anyway, whenever a beast offered to lift a tail an expectant group would take up a handy position at the rear. And this led to the extraordinary sight of a cattle feedlot with no dung to be seen. The cattle as usual dunged at random but the piggies cleaned that up. And then, as pigs do, they dunged in turn but only in their designated areas.

It made for very good house-keeping.

I tell you that in the hope that, like me, you will find it interesting, but also because it is relevant to what has been preoccupying me and my new pig fattening enterprise this week.

I know what it is like to farm with a thousand pounds an acre of overdraft and I know that I don't like it much. So, in considering taking on the pigs, I had a clear idea that it should involve the minimum of expen-diture and be possible with my present labour force, i.e. my-self. The point about those American pigs is that they don't need extra accommodation, they don't need fed at all and that they actually help keep the cattle feedlot tidy.

Well, I could hardly achieve such economy. For a start, I don't see the modern supermarket rushing to buy hoggs fed on cattle droppings; not with all the fuss that there has been over the use of cattle offal.

But the building was more or less idle. And the feeding system only involved buying two hoppers. We had the auger. We had the old bath. We had the grain cart to store the five tonne deliveries though we had to get a hatch put into the tail-door. And we had the door that blew off the barn last winter to act as the lid of our improvised feed bin.

I was showing Mossie my system and explaining with some pride that all I had to do to feed the two hundred was to open the tail-door of the cart, climb up the old feed barrier to put on the auger and the whole job would be done automati-cally.

I could see that he was do-ing his best to be impressed and that, uncharacteristically, he was trying to find a way to avoid hurting my feelings. Anyway his natural honesty worked and he said, in a pity-ing, almost kindly way, "Ye ken, Charlie, unless ye dae this richt, ye'll just get a sickener and ye'll be oot o' pigs efter this lot are finished."

I was hurt, of course, also

"of course" the hurt has grown as it has become more and more obvious that the great man is absolutely right.

Every part of my contraption was suspect at best. Like the auger which was all right for one hopper but wouldn't reach the other. So we got a piece of waving coil and taped it to the top. The idea was to fill one hopper and then shift the pipe to the other one. But waving coil is too rough and the nuts wouldn't run down it.

Then the auger had to be too high for the pigs to bite it so we had to put the bath up on blocks. But then the cart couldn't tip far enough to allow the nuts to run into the bath so we had to block the tractor up. Then again, with the low piggery roof, we couldn't get the cart tipped far enough to get more than the first tonne or so to run out.

So now my fully automatic, labour-saving system works like this. First yoke the tractor and take the cart outside. Tip right up to move the load to the back. Take inside again and block the cart up again. Then open the hatch, jump in between the hoppers and switch on the auger. Take a pail and while the auger is delivering to one hopper you fill the other manually, keeping an eye on the cart, and jumping down to adjust the flow every time the bath starts to run over. When the cart stops delivering go home in disgust and repeat the farce as soon as you have recovered your composure.

The grain bin is ordered and so is the feed line. So much for the low-cost enterprise that was going to keep me out of the clutches of the bankers. Better them than the boys with the white coats.

Wasting asset is recouped

DAWN HAS not yet cracked as I sit down to write up my diary. And yet I have already done what is probably the most important job of the day... I have taken the snowplough out to the end of the road to let The Breadwinner away to her job in Aberdeen.

It is a sad fact that there is nothing else I can do on the farm that will make anything like as much money as seeing her safely away to the real world of air-conditioned offices and positive cash flows. Mind you, having been my book-keeper for a couple of years in the early days nearly ruined her chances of such gainful employment.

The Breadwinner's first tentative step outside the house was a course at the college on farm accounts. She is quick with figures and found the course easy, passing with distinction, but only after a very rocky start. When working out their examples she could never get the right sign on the final figure... she always showed the 'profit' figure having a negative effect on the balance sheet. Doing the Little Ardo books had been a poor apprenticeship for a world in which the residual of a year's work was taken to be a profit.

Just how much reduced are our circumstances at Little Ardo was brought home in yet another way the other day, when I came across one of my father's balance sheets. At the tail end of the war he was able to buy the farm for four thousand pounds. And yet, after generating wages for six men, he was able to show a profit of three thousand... the farm was paying for itself in sixteen months and ensuring that the farmer could leave his working boots in the cupboard under the stairs.

Now The Farmer works all day, the most important job he does is to let The Breadwinner through the snow, and, with interest rates at sixteen per cent, he could work forever and never buy the farm.

Thank goodness it is bought already.

Before she took to bread-winning in a big way, Fiona went in for reproduction and was pretty good at that too. At least she was prolific though, it would be fair to say, the products have varied somewhat in quality.

We've two of each. That is, two Investments and two Wasting Assets.

The Investments were good girls and conscientious from the start. They were pretty too. "What a pretty girl you are," the oldest one was once told in the grocer's shop.

"I know." said the eight year old.

"And how do you ken that?" said the shopkeeper, much amused.

"Everybody keeps telling me," said the young Investment.

Anyway she and her sister went from strength to strength. Prize day at school made us ever-so proud. Then on to university, and honours degrees. Clearly these were to be Investments in a secure old age.

Unfortunately, life seemed to be a lot harder for the Wasting Assets. They didn't lack the brains, but they seemed to lack the vision to see that they were

really there to continue the line, to secure the succession and compete to see who could offer the old folks the biggest golden handshake to get us off to our retirement home. (We haven't found it yet, but it is called "Dunfermin".)

There were to be no graduation day parties for the Wasting Assets. In fact they disappeared days after they were age to leave school. Fed up of being bawled out by The Farmer for standing in the wrong place and moving the wrong way when herding, there was never any chance of them working on this (or any other) farm. In fact, even before they were old enough, they went off to the oil rigs.

At once they were earning more than The Farmer... seventeen years old and ten thousand a year. But these lads had never read about Mr. Micawber. Their recipe for happiness was "annual income ten thousand a year, annual expenditure ten thousand a year plus all you can borrow from your pals and screw out of the hire purchase."

Indeed, for The Wasting Assets, even that wasn't enough so they set off on even more lucrative pursuits, one as a pop star and the other as a multiple mine-host in the 'Costa Fortune'.

But there is still no sign of Mr. Micawber getting through.

Mind you, one of The Wasting Assets has not been entirely unproductive, for he has produced a Hope-for-the-Future. She has her mother's good looks and her father's optimism and easy nature.

She visited us last weekend and helped to make us realise that it isn't all in vain. At three years old she saw her first snow and her first two hundred pigs. Being only two feet nine high you'd think a level fall of seven inches (fully wellie height) would be a daunting prospect, but no. The Hope for the Future just kicked about amongst it with slight amusement but no great trauma. And when she saw the pigs she looked and looked and then said "Can you eat them?"

Now that surely was a hopeful remark. No nonsense about how cuddly they were, no panic and no cries about how dirty or how smelly they were... just practical good sense.

It may be that one Wasting Asset is in the process of producing a really good Investment of his own.

CAN YOU EAT THEM?

Turnball.

Support of nature's tornado

I MAY be the only one but I am really missing the snow.

There are few more exhilarating experiences than a walk in the freezing winter sun, the snow crackling and crumping underfoot, the air clear and the birds earnestly screeching and scratching for trifles in the cornyard.

And cold winters are much better for the work. You can get your bales of silage in without cutting great canals out of the fields and even bogging down in the mud. You can get the dung straight out of the courts and onto the fields and you can spread slurry as fast as the beasts can make it.

But there is another reason why I so enjoyed the snow with which the first half of February was blessed. The white blanket provided the perfect cover for the oil-seed rape and left the pigeons quite baffled. It was great not having to rush off every half an hour to scare doos.

It is just as well that we did get that break because things were becoming rather strained between me and Willie-the-Hunter, the poacher who helps me in my pigeon wars. I provide the cartridges and he comes with his gun to defend my crops. He doesn't get paid but he can sell the bag to the local game dealers.

Willie had expected a really remunerative season as Mitchell of Letham was advertising for pigeons at £1 a bird – the same as pheasants. But when the birds started to fly and Willie appeared with his first bagful the price was down to 30 pence. And now, with the air thick with them, John Bain is down to 20 pence.

But that's not what put the strain on my relationship with Willie the Hunter. It has always been difficult because the Hunter's main aim is to kill woodpigeons whereas mine is to keep them away from my oil-seed rape. Willie lies in wait and watches the pigeons grazing until he can get them so close that he can't miss. And even then he'll watch them eating at my precious crop until he has three or four of them all lined up and can hope for several birds per shot.

I, on the other hand, blaze away with both barrels as soon as the birds come into view in the hope that they will go away and graze my neighbour's fields. Willie doesn't like that.

The incompatibility of The Farmer and The Hunter reached new heights when we were watching the devils developing their flight one windy morning at the beginning of the month. There were about five hundred in the perennial rape, The Hunter's mouth was beginning to water and I was for blasting away to get them

shifted over to Hillies. All at once they took off. They landed again a hundred yards further away but soon all jumped up again.

No one had fired a shot. But the third time we saw what was upsetting them. Sweeping low over the dyke and across the field, not more than two feet above the crop, sped my hunter-killer – a sparrow hawk. He had clearly evaded the doos' radar for he was no more than twenty feet from the flock when they all took off again. The hawk didn't make a kill but this time they shifted to the next field… in amongst Arnybogs' turnips.

This was indeed a bonus for The Farmer; what could be better than having nature's Tor-

nado on my side. It was terribly 'green'... a 'biological' pesticide.

But The Hunter was furious... his sport and indeed his livelihood were threatened by this scab labour. It is very difficult to compete with one who will work for nothing.

We almost fell out over that hawk. I was busy thinking about feeding him to keep him on my land so making sure he didn't move to Arnybogs and scare the doos back here. Willie on the other hand was laying plans to shoot the creature.

Anyway, the snow came and gave us a breather from one another and Willie saw that, annoying as the hawk was, it wasn't worth going to jail for.

The break gave me a chance to visit the Perth bull sales for the first time since 1986. I've two already so I had no use for a bull but I thought I might buy a cow or two at the dispersal of the adult portion of the Moncur herd of Simmentals.

I always get a thrill when I settle at the ringside at a pedigree sale. I could be in for a bargain or I could be like the crofter who had rather too much whisky and found himself the proud owner of a cow which cost £6000. I often wonder what his wife said to him when he got that cow home.

Anyway, I did quite a bit of waving but didn't succeed in buying. I came close twice. Once, as it looked as though I was to get an old banger for £1500, a new bidder appeared from nowhere. It turned out to be Stephen Mackie who is not only a neighbour but a cousin.

And my other near thing was the fault of another relative. He had once told an auctioneer that he wouldn't take a penny less than a hundred pounds for his bull. The auctioneer made a start, taking bids quickly from here and there. However bidding stuck at £98.

"Ach, jist sell 'im," said my progenitor at last.

"Be quiet you fool. I havna' got a bid yet."

Now, I remembered that story when I was bidding for a cow and calf. I couldn't see anybody bidding against me so I dropped out.

It had been an unworthy thought. The cow was knocked down to a very small man standing behind a very big one.

Aversion to dogs and cars

I LOVE the farm and I even love farming... a little. But there are two pieces of farm equipment for which I have no love at all.

I may even be unique in this respect, for most farmers seem to like their dogs very much and love their cars way beyond the call of duty. I know farms where you can't see the fire for the dogs and I've known several farmers who have bought a shiny new car in the year in which they called in the receiver or gave up the struggle to keep their creditors from so doing.

As a student of Freudian psychology, I put my aversion to cars and dogs down to traumas in early childhood.

Take dogs. At four years old I thought of dogs, as I thought of

the whole world, as things of wonder, put there by a loving God for me to play with. This incautious philosophy was in place when I espied a Scottie bitch in the close of the farm at which I was a most willing refugee from Hitler.

I ran over to the dog and discovered, in the most painful of ways, that the Scottie is a proud and independent breed which can take ill to people who have not been properly introduced. It didn't quite break the skin but I can still see the curious blue tooth marks deep in my pink wrist.

I have no recollection of being brave or of getting any sympathy from my grandparents who were always very matter-of-fact. But, despite their lack of fuss, I have been left with a considerable respect for dogs which persists almost fifty years later.

And you would think that that Scottie had told the whole dog kingdom of the incident for, if dogs make me nervous, I certainly have the same effect on them. I can go into a room in which there is a dog sleeping at the fire. It will immediately start to snarl. The owners will apologise and I'll be quite nice about it while making it clear that I think they should train

their dog to know better. And all the while, I know that there is nothing wrong with the dog that my disappearance wouldn't cure.

So what about my aversion to cars?

Well, it was when I was seventeen and drove a 1936 ex-post office van. I was proud of my first four-wheeler and had it painted a rather dashing sky blue with shocking pink mudguards. It still had the wire grill that had separated the postie from his letters and I had her proclaimed in neat lettering 'The Hen Coupe'.

In an amazing feat of endurance I had driven the Coupe all the way to Devon for a cricket tour. With a top speed of forty miles per hour, it had taken me three days to drive down, and I was nearing the end of the second day of the return journey when it happened.

I had made very good time and, as dusk and a smir of rain were falling, I had crossed the Kincardine Bridge and was anxiously peering into the gathering gloom in search of the road that would take me to Kinross and home.

In the feeble beam I saw the sign when it was upon me; "Alloa left, Kinross straight on". What I had not seen was the part of the sign that indicated a roundabout.

I turned fatefully right and was proceeding round this gentle left-hand curve when round the corner, on what I had thought was my side of the road, came a large black car. The large black car stopped, but, my brakes being inadequate to the occasion the Hen Coupe did not.

At that time I was used to things which went wrong turning out to be my fault. So I was not surprised to find I was sitting on a roundabout and facing the wrong way.

And that was not all I was facing. For out of the passenger seat of the large, black and shiny car jumped a big and very irate man. I could see immediately that this was a man who was used to being taken seriously. "Do you know who ah am?" he bellowed. And without waiting for a reply (which was considerate) "Ah'm the superintendent of Alloa Police."

"Oh really," said I, impressed. "I'm Charlie Allan."

The super was unimpressed and guided me off the road to await the squad car which would give me "the high jump".

Things looked black for our hero. And they did not readily improve.

As we waited he asked me why I had made what he recognised had been a mistake. I told him I'd been driving for thirteen hours and was tired, that my windscreen wipers weren't working except when I put my hand out of the window and waggled them, and that my lights being so weak I hadn't had time to read the sign properly.

It was then that I learned that, while lies are for very special occasions, it can be foolish to volunteer the whole truth. I was charged with driving while incapable through exhaustion, with faulty lights and windscreen wipers. And that was before the squad car came.

"What speed were you doing?"

"I couldn't say exactly cos my speedo's on the blink."

"Did you sound your horn?"

"No, it doesna' work."

That was two more charges and I ended up with a total of thirteen. A pretty formidable start for a seventeen year-old.

Mind you, I wasn't all eejit even then. As we waited for the police car I went and apologised to the super's wife for spoiling her evening. She in-

41

vited me into the car and got my life-story. As I left to speak to the coppers she said "I'll do my best for you, son."

I think she must have done, for I was only summoned for bad brakes and ignoring a traffic signal... surely a bargain at six pounds.

Policy is cheap old bangers

I WAS telling you last week about my aversion to two common tools of the farmer's trade. I attributed that to my first dog biting the hand that tried to pat it, and my first set of four wheels which lead me the wrong way round a roundabout and into collision with the superintendent of Alloa Police.

After I had bid the super a warm good-evening I set off for the north with a heavy heart and a heavy list of thirteen charges.

At last, and thankful to have no further additions to my charge sheet, I eventually made Little Ardo. And just at the head of the short brae that leads down to the farm the engine cut out. I free-wheeled the old 1936 ex-post office Morris Minor van down through the close and onto the scrap yard. Despite many efforts the 'Hen Coupe' never turned another wheel in earnest.

It was an ignominious end to my thousand mile safari and there was worse to come. Perhaps it is the key to my distrust of cars. It had been bad enough being humiliated by the Alloa Police but it was what had happened to my investment that most put me off cars.

You see I had laid out no less than £25 to buy her, not six months earlier and the depreciation was horrendous. I eventually got an Irish dealer, who came round selling strawberry nets, to give me a pound and a free net for her, and the grieve's wife gave me 20 Capstan Full Strength for the travelling rug.

The Automobile Association tell me that the depreciation on the sorts of cars most farmers drive are even worse. I refer, of course, to Skodas and Ladas. In the first four years they reckon a car loses half it's value... as much as thirty per cent in the first year.

And of course it's a serious financial loss for those few who go up-market. A new Range Rover costs just under twenty-one thousand plus just over five thousand of tax, so you lose that for a start. You can sometimes do better if you buy something like a Rolls Royce, a Merc. or a BMW which may be in short supply, but, according to the A.A.'s Roy Staunton, "It's an unfortunate fact of life that most of us who buy a car are going to lose money".

Now, my philosophy of car purchase is to lose as little as possible. I could go out and buy myself a modest car for ten thousand (some farmers do, you know). That would lose £1250 per annum in depreciation in the first four years. At current interest rates the money tied up would cost another £1650 and the comprehensive insurance could easily be another £500 per annum... and a good deal more for anyone who crashes into the superintendent of Alloa Police.

That adds up to £10 a day before you've put petrol in the damned thing or shown it to your unfriendly neighbourhood garage.

His car must be just about the worst investment the average farmer ever makes.

Not me though. I once had an almost new Audi which I enjoyed until it was no longer nearly new and the chassis broke on it's way into a ditch. Since then I have invested in wheels much more economically.

It started with and old Vauxhall for £100 with four months tax on it. That ran without major problems for three years until my wife refused to travel in it. I then raced up market and paid four hundred for a Skoda. And when I came back from Kenya two years ago I bought a Ford Cortina estate car for six hundred and, for my Sunday car, a Volkswagen Golf which I was already borrowing to leave in a field as a scarecrow.

Now the sums on those cars average out at depreciation £100, insurance (third party only) £80 and capital tied up £50. That's a saving of over three thousand a year... *per car*. And better than that, my cars never depreciate fully as I can use them to scare the doos off the rape when they finally fail their M.O.T..

There are, I have to admit, disadvantages to driving old cars... I've had to give up any idea of standing for high office in the Farmer's Union, for example, and I wouldn't even think of ordinary membership of the Tory party.

Anyway, I'm sticking to my policy of cheap old bangers and, I venture to suggest, there are many old men, broke today, who would still be farmers had they done likewise. It is the single easiest way to improve a balance sheet.

On the other hand I may have to overcome my prejudice against dogs. The kids were never much good at being gates and they've left anyway, and the Breadwinner is never here. I have no staff now so I really will need to sell the stock or get a dog.

Mind you it is possible to get by without one. I remember when my father was renting out grass at Little Ardo and the dairyman, who had fifty heifers here recovering from their winter, wanted them in for worming. Four men chased these bitches up and down the field all morning before retiring to the pub for a pint, a rest and their lunch.

Now all this had been witnessed by the grieve who had been over forty years on the place and was by no means pleased that his precious acres were now on the market. James Low determined to top off a most entertaining morning by putting one over the interlopers.

For some reason he had an old foghorn, and when the herds had disappeared for refreshment he sat down behind the dyke and started to blow. The heifers came running to see what it was and, finding the gate open, trotted out and up to the steading where the bugler was able to shut the gate.

I don't have a fog-horn or old Jimmy's cunning so I'm afraid it will have to be a dog.

March 18, 1991

Zebra and giraffe problem

IF LIKE me, you are finding it hard to make a living selling cattle on the hoof for a hundred and ten pence a kilo, you should spare a thought for the farmer I visited last week. He is having to twist the butcher's arm right up his back to get above 14 pence a kilo.

That's the going rate for steers just outside Nairobi. You see The Breadwinner, who has always wanted to go back to Africa, finally came up with the fare, and there being little doing on the farm just now, The Farmer agreed to a holiday with her in the sun.

And so it was that we landed in Kenya, right on the equator only fourteen hours after leaving the snows of Little Ardo.

It was a change entirely for the better. The sun shone out of a cloudless sky almost all of every day and yet, being over a thousand feet higher than Ben Nevis, Nairobi was always pleasantly cool out of the direct sunshine.

We stayed in the Nairobi Club and visited her sister establishments set up throughout the Rift Valley by the white settlers.

It was a delightful experience. It is all still there; the smiling service, the large pepper steaks for £1.50, the excellent beer at 30 pence a pint, the swimming pools, the golf courses, tennis and squash courts, and the cricket pitches. The members reflect rather less light than they did when Kenya was one of the last bastions of the Raj, but that is all to the good. I confess that I was proud of the marvellous facilities the settlers had set up and gladdened by the way that they have been kept up by today's Kenyans.

I can't tell you all about our trip but I must tell you about our visit to my old friend Ole Sein. He has a two thousand acre farm on the Northern Serengeti just outside Nairobi. This is ranch land where for centuries the world's most dedicated cattlemen have led a semi-nomadic existence and lived entirely on their beasts.

And I do mean entirely. The cow provides dung to make the house, skins to make the clothes and the bedding, milk to drink and meat or blood to eat on feast days. These herdsmen also have the cow as the centre-piece of their religion, for they believe that when God made the cow he gave it to them... a very convenient philosophy which meant that anybody else seen with a cow must have stolen it and that provides perfect justification for stealing it 'back'.

For Ole Sein is one of the famous and feared Maasai. The tribe the whites used to say could never be tamed and whom the Kenyan government are having the greatest diffi-culty bullying into the twenti-eth century.

While many of his family and most of his tribe are cling-ing to the old way of life as best they can, Ole Sein has settled down. He is an educated man who lives in a stone-built house, eats vegetables, keeps his cows on fenced land and even sends his children to Uni-versity in the United States.

But he surely can't be put-ting his children through school off his cows... not at today's prices anyway. While we've had the stuffing knocked out of our markets by 'food scares' Ole Sein's troubles are mostly put down to Saddam's war and the American tourists' poor ge-ography.

The Kenyans expect some half a million Americans a year to give them a hand to chew their way through the beef they are so good at producing. But despite attempts to show them that Kenya is nowhere near the Gulf they have stayed at home almost to a man. So Ole Sein is glad to get 14 pence a kilo for his pure Simmental steers.

Like all farmers he is happy to blame the butchers for profi-teering so I went looking for the evidence. I went to our old butcher Mzee Gilani but could see no unnecessary inflation there. He is at £1.25 for silver-side, £1.50 for sirloin and £4.00 for fillet *per kilo*.

And Ole Sein has other problems. Like me and my pi-geons he has a problem with pests. But his problems are big-ger than mine in two ways. First, he is not allowed by Ken-yan law to shoot or otherwise dispose of his pests and sec-ondly they are huge. For Ole Sein plays host to a herd of a hundred zebras and about fifty giraffes.

They used to be kept down to some extent by the leopards but those have been scared away by the pack of six horrendous alsatian dogs he has for security about the place.

So the grass has to support more than the cows in the shade of the Ngong Hills. There are great plans to drive the zebras out through a gate at the south side of the farm, though the next farmer could be forgiven if he drove them back again, (just like Mossie and me with the doos).

But Ole Sein is at his wits end as to what to do with the giraffes. The eight foot fence round his ranch is no barrier to them. They rear up and elegantly lower their front legs on the other side. For a moment they are astride the fence. Then they kick up their back legs, step smartly forward on their front ones and they're in.

I'm back with the pigeons now and despite the attentions of one of the Wasting Assets while we were away it is not before time.

But I must remember Ole Sein and try not to complain too much about my lot here. When

I got home there was a cheque for ten stots sold at 110 pence per kilo, another for a previous lot of beef special premium worth another five pence. Then there was a cheque for my Hill Livestock Compensation and another for my Beef Cow Subsidy.

My old Maasai friend manages without all that... but then his people always have.

Hamish's gallant stand against authority still remains intact

I SOLD the wheat this week. Not a bad trade too though it still seems to be rising. I got £128 a tonne compared to £117 last year. And, with all but four of my 1989 calves away, that has given me what I call my 'overdraft window'; the brief moment at the end of winter when there is money in the bank.

Of course it is an entirely false position. An underdraft is only made possible by the patience of my creditors who will have to be paid soon. Then there is all the spring work to be done and paid for as well as grazing cattle to be bought.

Nevertheless, I am savouring the moment. I make little excuses to visit the bank at least once a day and pretend to consult the manager about an investment policy for my surplus

PRIDE COMETH BEFORE THE CREDITORS ARE PAID!

BANK

Turnbull.

funds. It's all a charade of course but I enjoy being bowed in and bowed out again. It makes a welcome change from the days when Little Ardo carried £1000 an acre of debt and the 'overdraft window' was the few weeks in the year when the figures in red were below their limit.

Mind you, Big Hamish reckons it's a disaster to have money in the bank. He likes to have his cash on wheels and is pretty successful in keeping his borrowings up to and beyond his limit. He is currently wrestling with the decision on spending thirty thousand on an even bigger Ford tractor and he's found an additional argument for borrowing.

You see Hamish is not just a farmer of renown. He is also a man of principle. And his iron principles would not let him pay his poll tax. At least they wouldn't let him pay the first year of the tax... for some reason he has paid the second year.

Anyway, the authorities have got the power to apply directly to Hamish's bankers for recovery of the tax due. They have that power and they have tried to exercise it but they have no power to negotiate higher overdraft limits on Hamish's part. As he is hard up against the limit the banker had to refuse the order to pay up and, poll tax still unpaid, our man's gallant stand against authority is still intact.

Hamish is delighted. He has another week to pay "or else". Or else what? No one seems to know, but it is rumoured that Big Hamish has plans to take to the hills in his £27,000 digger and dare them to take him.

Another of the discussion group has been starring. The Red Rooster is just back from investigating the land market in East Germany. A pal of his from America has just rented some thousands of acres of formerly state run land at £12.50 an acre. Now that East Germany is in the Common Market they can produce grain there and sell it into intervention.

It's good land and apparently there is very little competition for it. The East Germans have had all the stuffing knocked out of them by forty years of collectivisation, and the West German farmers are so small, and so busy building Volkswagens in their spare time, that they aren't interested.

Clearly what is needed is some Scottish barley-barons to come in and show them how it should be done. In fact I think the ideal thing to get capitalism going again in the East would be a combination of Scotsmen and Kikuyus from Kenya. The latter are the most enterprising farmers I know. Perhaps the best example of that is the world's longest and thinnest farm. It belongs to a Kikuyu and is situated between the carriageways of the main road from Nairobi to Thika.

The German hosts had got the thing off to a suitable start by announcing "Ve are paying everysing except ze girls und ze bar". That was wise for, though they might have chanced the girls, the bar would have been a sizable contract. Anyway, the Rooster's party sailed round East Germany on a sea of white wine looking for prairies at £12.50 an acre.

But they came home empty handed. Like so many good things before them, the cheap opportunities in the East have their snags.

The land was there alright but it seemed that only Germans were getting it. The Rooster's American who was successful turned out to have a German granny and could speak the language.

And inability to speak German (or, as he so Britishly put it, "the fact that the Gerries canna speak English") had been a big handicap. The Rooster had wished he'd had Mossie there for, on a previous trip, he, though quite untutored in the language, had spoken German to great effect after ten pints or so... and that was most of the time.

Meanwhile, back at Little Ardo, we have been using the overdraft window to do a little gentle improving. We've had the readymix lorry to fill in a rough bit round the grain drier area. It cost us a bit each year in spillage so I suppose there is an economic reason for it but really the big bonus of the concrete is the improved look of the place.

Laying that concrete gave fuel to my long held view that experts are pretty useless.

You see the squad was The Farmer, Potions the chemist, one of the Wasting Assets who is between jobs again, and an expert. He was my neighbour Gowkie, who as well as being a hill-farmer is a time-served mason.

We all did our best and deferred to Gowkie's direction. The job done we admired our handiwork and remarked on how small the puddle in the low bit was compared with some we'd seen. Gowkie, as the expert, took a particularly active part in the post-mortem with much shaking of the head and gesticulation.

Then, just like any other expert, he absent mindedly walked right into it. And not just one step but three.

April 1, 1991

Spring magic of cows out at grass

BY THE time you read this it will be springtime in Aberdeenshire. Of course the wind may be whipping the snow down at us from the North Pole, but history will show that, in 1991 the spring day was on Monday the first of April.

You could be forgiven for thinking that a cruel 'April Fool', for traditionally we don't let the cattle out until the first of May. So it was in my father's time. On May-day, after they had been a six months tied in stalls, the neck-bands were loosed and we let them run.

The cows had never shown any discontent with their winter quarters though the regime was hardly stimulating. They were milked and mucked twice a day, twice a day they shared a barrow load of neeps with their stallmate and got a bucketful of dry mash. That would be big if they were a high yielder or were one of the baillie's favourites, and would be small if they were poor milkers or had kicked the cattleman recently.

Apart from a comb once a day and the occasional kick to get them up for inspection, that was how our cows spent half their lives.

No wonder then, that the spring day was one of such excitement. They say that battery hens offered their freedom will cower back in their pens rather than risk the unknown. But the cow has no agoraphobia.

Watched anxiously by the baillie, the grieve and my father, outside they went, tentatively at first and then at a smart walk. Down the road and into the field at the trot. And then, when they got off the hard stony road and onto the soft grass their joy was unrestrained. They kicked their hind legs up like broncos bucking at a rodeo, challenged each other to mock head to heads and charged off, the great udders slapping from side to side, to explore the farthest corners of their expanded universe.

It always struck me as a

54

wonder that, even on the spring day, when milking-time came, the cows would walk quietly back up the road to the steading and back into their own stalls to wait patiently for the cattleman to tie them up again. They seemed to know that this time it would not be for six months.

The reason for letting them out at the beginning of May was that there would be plenty of grass by then and there is no feed for cattle like spring grass. Of course the excitement and the change of feeding meant a drop in yields for a start but, as soon as the food outside was better than the food inside, out they would go.

And it's still the same philosophy today. The reason we have put the cattle out a month early is that the few wisps of wet grass and last year's foggage are better feeding than what's left for feeding then inside.

On April Fool's Day we will be clean out of winter keep. Rain, hail or sunshine, spring comes to Little Ardo this day.

I can only tell you about this because my father, the old grieve and the baillie, are all dead. If they are witnesses to my improvidence, at least it will be a year or two before they can tell me to my face what they think of my stewardship of the family farm.

Of course the spring day won't be such an event this year as it was thirty years ago. All our cattle are loose-housed now so they are used to a degree of freedom even when they are inside. And then, with the poor snecks I employ and the willing rather than accomplished help I tend to get about the place, it will be an unlucky beast indeed which has not had at least one taste of freedom during the winter.

Nevertheless, if we get anything of a day, I'll enjoy April the first. The sight of cattle getting out to the grass remains one of the enduring pieces of magic on the farm.

Sadly though, the profitability of the farm is doomed to depend again on the combinable crops rather than on the livestock. And there at least the picture is mixed. The barley and wheat are looking well though one field has a slight manganese deficiency and everything is three weeks behind last year. The rape is looking thin where it nearly all blew away last back-end and in the sixteen acres or so cleared by pigeons.

My crops consultant tells me we can still prosper if we do everything right from here on and that means getting the manure on at the right time and the right sprays at the right times.

Unfortunately, ability in those departments really measures the difference between a punter like me and crackshots like Mossie and the Red Rooster.

They really study the thing. They go to discussion groups, lectures and open days, and argue the toss with one another about the virtues of sprays and sprayers till the cows come home. Mind you Mossie has seen through the uneconomics of the cow and doesn't have any.

For all our heroes' academic diligence they have both learnt most from the University of Trial and Error. And though people come from far and near to learn from their experience it isn't always easy to get them to part with the knowledge so expensively won.

One crackshot brought his green wellies up from the south recently. Having told the boys all he knew about sprays, and litres to the hectare he would hold a clinic at the Red Rooster's. The crops were impressive to the point of embarrassment. But the guest could make nothing of the explanation of the treatment in pints per acre.

56

"Na, na," the Rooster had said. "We hinna got roon tae hectacres yet."

And the poor consultant learned even less when viewing Mossie's burgeoning acres. "We just give it three tins of this and a coffee mug of that to the fill... of the sprayer."

Advancing with riot shields

THIS MORNING I have a shambles to report.

You see my environmental porkers are ready for market and on Wednesday we loaded ninety. It was not an experience I want to repeat.

You will recall that we got two hundred of these pigs which are specially bred to survive in a series of what the authors portray as 'natural' environments. The piggies are born outside in little tin arcs and have a few weeks scurrying about in the mud or snow. Then they are reared in sawdust and finished in straw courts.

I have no doubt that the system is worth a try, not least because the consumers are turning in ever-increasing numbers to food which they believe is produced in ways that preserve the animals welfare and even its dignity. The trouble is that, while enjoying all that freedom, the pigs also acquire a set of skills which can make loading a nightmare.

They are unbelievably fast and weighing fifteen stone with a centre of gravity about nine inches off the ground they are hard to stop. Some have even developed a body swerve and sidestep that would do justice to Phil Bennet.

Of course we were not without weapons of our own. We each had a plywood board and Potions the Chemist, Peter the Pigger from the buyers, and myself went into the pen to wile out the fattest ones.

The concept was fair enough. We would advance towards the piggies with our boards held in front of us like riot police with their shields, and usher the fattest ones to the gate in twos and threes. There the Armstrong (the man we hire for such emergencies from the Buchan Machinery Ring) was charged with making sure none that weren't ready escaped and that none who had already been selected got back.

We had some successes, of course, but I'm afraid we had many frustrations. We might

58

have been in a ten acre field. There was the sheer speed of these consumer-friendly pigs. And the flimsiness of our pig boards. In the end of the day, if piggie didn't want to go to market all it had to do was take a run at the pig boards. And the discipline of my troops was no better than that of the riot police. If you recall them charging individually and blindly at a disappearing wall of students you'll have some idea of our performance.

Eventually we had enough pigs extracted… not the ones we wanted, but enough. Then all we had to do was to get them to go out of the shed and into the float.

The plan was to herd them out in fours to the loading bank. There they would walk up a chute thing we had borrowed from Mossie. The driver would number them while one of the Wasting Assets would take over and herd them up the chute.

Our problems were just starting.

The piggies had now learned that they were in command and the first thing they were against was leaving the shed. We had obviously been far too good to them. They wanted back to their straw and their endless supply of delicious nuts.

So it was at the door of the shed that they learned another trick. They could hurdle our pig

59

boards which were no more than two feet high. And when we tried to combat that by raising the boards you could be sure that another piggie would take the chance to dive out underneath.

But the problems at the door of the shed were as nothing compared to getting them to go up Mossie's chute. It was metal and clanged when they stood on it. And it wasn't stable which didn't add to the piggie's sense of security.

I don't suppose those pigs would ever have been loaded had it not been for the Wasting Asset. He's here for what he had hoped would be a holiday from his job of running a nightclub in Tenerife. That job involves a number of skills including bouncing and he ended up bouncing our ninety into the float.

The Wasting Asset may yet bring honour to the family as the All Scotland Pig-Wrestling Champion. And I am certainly going to offer that day's work to Guinness for their Book of Records. We only loaded five pigs per man-hour.

I reckon the going rate for work like that would be about a fiver so that is a pound a pig.

And the company only pays me four pounds a pig for keeping them for ten weeks. Clearly that will never do... especially with the remaining one hundred and ten to load next Wednesday.

We put up the tail door of the float and immediately set about making sure of a quiet time next Wednesday. Twenty tons of stone gatherings and two cubic metres of ready-mix concrete have made a race track and loading bank direct from the pigs pen. On Monday we open their pen gate and give them two days to snuffle about and mark the territory with their familiar smells. When it comes to Wednesday they will trot out and into the float without any bother. And if there should be any reluctance to enter the float they wont be able to jump over our new pig boards. We hope.

We are always learning. And from the experience of these pigs I have learned that, if anyone comes and tells me I can diversify my farming without any capital outlay on specialised equipment, I should prepare for a disappointment. The only hope we have in farming is to tool up properly to do the job right and with the minimum of hassle.

Vauxhall Cavalier missing

JAMES LOW, the grieve who terrorised this farm for forty four of the years between 1930 and 1980, was a potential Prime Minister with far more important things to do. There were only two ways to do a job, the wrong way and Jimmy's way. He didn't suffer fools for long and once told an excellent tractorman who had made a slight error "Man Jock, if ye jist had a bit mair sense ye could be a half-wit".

That sort of attitude didn't endear the grieve to everyone. But that was only fair for he didn't give a damn as long as the place was looking well and the work was a few days ahead of our neighbours.

James Low came to Little Ardo when it was one of old Maitland Mackie's ten or so outfarms. And that meant that he had not only to do better than his neighbours but also than the grieves at the other farms in the

Mackie empire.

The rivalry was bitter and for some reason James had a particular ill-will about the management team at Westertown of Rothienorman (now farmed by Old-Man Mackie's other grandson Maitland the Third... the Vice-Chairman of the National Farmer's Union of Scotland).

The grieve used to tell me that the men at Westertown would get in their tractors and drive over the hill where they could get a read of the papers undisturbed. And he poured particular scorn on the occasion when a heifer had been smothered by a falling soo of hay and they had never missed it.

I tell you all that because the story of Westertown's heifer has been brought up to date, only this time it was a car. Old Jimmy would fairly have enjoyed this new story and he'd have told just everybody.

But Jimmy's away now so the job has been done by *Big Farm Weekly*.

And 'Big Farm' is right for Westertown these days. It has two hundred employees between farming, manufacturing ice cream and retailing. And it has 'executives'. One of those, recently appointed, is called the General Manager for Finance and Administration. When Ashley Thom was checking on his new empire he found the heifers were all there but that a Vauxhall Cavalier was missing from the car fleet. Chairman, Maitland Mackie, claimed no knowledge of it and confirmed that, on this occasion, none of the family had borrowed it.

Luckily, and before the police were called, Maitland suddenly remembered that he had left it at the airport when he had returned from a trip to London by a different route. It had been there for three weeks.

Meanwhile, back at Little Ardo, our General Manager for Finance and Administration joined the rest of the staff for the second instalment of loading our robust consumer-friendly pigs for market.

It so often happens in life, that as one door closes another door slams in your face.

We had spent most of the week before making a pig-tight loading race and bank to avoid a repeat of last week's rodeo. We cut down on the staff too, in the hope that fewer people would excite less of a fever. Peter the Pig who as buyer was the only one who understood pig psychology, went into the pen of 110 and expertly ushered the fat ones out individually. They'd had a day of wandering out of the pen and along the race so that that was all familiar to them and, with me guarding the gate, we soon had the 50 ready for the float.

It arrived twenty minutes late and was at least twenty feet too long. They had sent the biggest artic they had to pick up fifty pigs from a farm which was designed for the horse cart.

He came roaring down to the pigs shed and off the delicate rim of concrete. There the driver couldn't find reverse because, he said, it wasn't level. When we had hauled the lorry out with the digger, and he had found the missing gear the driver then failed to find any wheelgrip and we had to pull him backwards to where he should have turned in the first place.

Now, I have every sympathy with the driver. I can't back an artic either even when the air brakes aren't jamming-on all the time. But then I'm not trying to earn my living as a lorry driver.

When we got him turned the lorry then set off to reverse down to the piggery again but missed the loading bank. I pulled him up again and he missed again.

After two and a quarter hours the driver gave up in disgust. I pulled him up the hill again and waved him goodbye. The pigs were returned to their pen. We would try again in five days time.

My two hours in the glass-free cab of my digger had given the lie to the idea that the attraction of farming lay in it's way of life. I settled into the bath to defrost.

When the first phone call came it was the floater's office. Who was going to pay his £100 for the waste of his lorry's time? I didn't say a thing about sending a juggernaut to do a job that was better suited to a barrow or anything tactless.

The second phone call told me that another more modest float was on it's way and would I just get the fifty out of the pen again.

I think the pigs took pity on me. They came out of the pen willingly and up the ramp and into the lorry like the happy chosen boarding the Ark.

The whole job didn't take half an hour. I think we've cracked it.

April 22, 1991

First with W.C. in the county

IT HAS been an emotional week.

Five years ago I shed tears of rage and humiliation when the minister of this parish told me that, as my father had not been a member of the church, we could not hold a service there in honour of his memory. This week I was back again, asking the new minister if he would conduct a service for my mother.

There were tears again. There are tears now as I write. But these are tears of gratitude. For the minister told me then that, as long as he was in Methlick, the Church would belong to all his parishioners.

I don't really care for public shows of grief but what can you do when your shoulders start shaking in the middle of the 23 Psalm? There is nowhere to hide.

So that's another generation who have farmed on this hill away and the Farmer is now an orphan.

In 1857 my great grandfather William Yull built the old barn. It has an engraved stone to prove it. And his son gave Little Ardo the first water-closet in the county... the tenant of Little Ardo had a W.C. before the Lords of Aberdeen to whom he paid his rent.

My grandfather bought the place in 1920, planted an eight acre wood, put up a dairy byre and a tattie shed you can't get a tractor into nowadays and a piggery which, being all of 146 feet long was a wonder in it's time and is still fit for 400 fatteners.

So what is my parents contribution to the farm which gave them a living which was often generous and always adequate?

In 1945 they built 'the new barn'. It was made necessary by the need for a continuous supply of fresh straw for the dairy cows. It allowed us to get the mill inside so that we could thrash in all weathers.

That was a great innovation. It had shakers that took the straw from the mill and deposited it through a series of trapdoors for storing. And the chaff from the mill was blown along a series of nine inch pipes either to the chaff house or straight into the cattle court where the heifers were wintered.

And the great thing about the new barn was it's height. Even now we could get big tractors into the place if we had any and the digger goes in with ease even with the back-acter on. The trouble starts though when those big machines are in the barn. It's walls are only a single brick thick. One touch from the digger and the wall cracks... one real skelp and the whole lot will be a pile of rubble.

Luckily my parents' contribution to the family farm lies not in the building they put up. With great foresight they tried to make Little Ardo a fine place at which to live.

They it was who cemented the close, and they tormented the old County Council for years to come and tar the three quarters of a mile of the 'Loans', the road that leads in about. My mother finally melted the councillors' hearts with a letter which said, "The road is now so bad that we fear that when we die it will be impossible for the hearse to get here to remove our remains."

When my mother and I came here at the tail end of the war there were a dozen or so battered trees at the top of this hill. But my parents have surrounded the old house with woods which shelter us in the storms and are homes for wildlife that wouldn't have dreamt of coming here in the nineteen-forties.

The farmhouse at Little Ardo was built in the eighteenth century when they knew a bit about line and about style. The Victorians had spoiled it somewhat by replacing the traditional twelve paned windows by four panes. Those might have been easier to clean but, when my mother put back the small panes, it was the remaking of the old house.

She had five brothers and sisters, each of whom had been put into a farm by their father, old Maitland Mackie. Now those siblings regarded themselves as farmers rather than landowners and one by one they took the opportunity to finance their farming by selling the land. It always looked crazy to have an overdraft at ten per cent when you could be paying rent at three so selling always looked right. But, for whatever reason I do not know, my parents never sold and though one of her brother's families has

since bought the land back, there came a time when only one of old Maitland's farms remained in the family, and that was Little Ardo.

Holding on to the land was a crucial contribution to keeping the place in the family. I find it difficult enough to hold on as an owner-occupier and I would not be able to if I had to pay rent.

But strangely, my parents' outstanding contributions to the place are not commercial or residential, but literary. My father's books *Farmer's Boy* and *The North East Lowlands of Scotland* are classics. And my mother, who we buried last week, has also made a contribution which will last.

In her late years she published a volume of poems called *A Little Piece of Earth*. They have no rhymes but many rhythms and good reasons. They tell of old age, of heritage and are sceptical of the cult of youth.

One of my favourites would almost do as an epitaph:

Once I was a young girl
Weeping on a rented bed

Now I am an old woman
With two public rooms
And three bedrooms
All empty

And I cannot weep.

Hiding our shame from our neighbours

I SUPPOSE we shouldn't be surprised by the foul weather. We have, after all, a whole vocabulary specially for describing it. This is the Gab o' May.

Now, before you protest that it is not yet May, I can tell you, on the authority of the Scottish National Dictionary that the Gab o' May is "a spell of stormy weather about the beginning of May". And it is about the beginning of May.

It sure has been stormy with winds which have made spraying impossible and even the application of fertilisers has been interrupted. We've had sleet most days and occasional teuchat's storms. That's a late snow storm called after the green plovers which return in March to scream and wheel over our spring work here in the north-east.

Whatever you call it, the weather is getting the blame for the crops being late and looking no better than fair. We do have some rape looking really well and one field looking by far the worst I have seen on Little Ardo since my father tried half a field of maize in the 1940s. That was a total failure from every point of view except that of the rooks who cleaned every single seed. It is the only case of which I have ever heard where a farmer achieved zero germination.

It might have been better for our worst field to have been worse. Then at least we might have ploughed it up and sown some spring barley. But we've let it go too long now.

The September gale blew most of the seedlings right out of the ground and there is about one half of the field where there are no more than a quarter of the plants we need to hide our shame... right beside the road.

It's no good saying "but it's quite good at the far side".

My neighbours are of

course enjoying this disgrace hugely and I try to divert their attention by pointing out our field of perennial rape. You see we are innovators again.

In the backend we were hit by some uncertain weather and some absolutely certain inefficiency as a result of which we failed to get all the rape that we would have liked sown. But one of the fields which had performed so well last year came to the rescue.

The Byre Park, as we call it, had given us 33 cwts of rape seed to the acre and having absorbed a huge middenful of dung, proceeded to produce a quite luxuriant breer without us having to sow it.

My crops consultant had never heard of perennial rape except for the man whose field of setaside produced a fair crop of volunteers. That man asked the Department of Agriculture what to do as regards topping the crop. The advice was that anything that would cut it down would be acceptable.

Now the most obvious machine to use as a topper was, of course, the combine. Would that be acceptable? Eventually the department agreed provided the resulting rape seed was 'dumped'. So our friend 'dumped' it in his grain store.

That gave him five cwts to the acre without paying a penny piece for cultivation, seeds or sprays.

So if that man could get five cwts, how much better might my crop do with a bit of tender loving care?

On went the compound fertilisers and the sprays. It suffered a terrible die-back during the winter but it has been sprayed twice and it has come away so strongly that I darednot plough it up for spring barley. It is sink or swim now for the first crop of perennial rape in the north east.

And it may very well be 'sink' for there is a lot of light leaf spot on it and, not knowing how much to allow for the four inches of muck we put on in the back-end, we may have put on too little nitrogen at 120 units... at any rate it looks a bit pale.

On the livestock front, I now have the final figures for my first race of outdoor pigs which we are fattening for Grampian Country Pork. For keeping the two hundred fatteners for an average of 68 days I am to get £4.25 per piggie.

They have turned pig meal into pork at the rate of 2.82 pounds of feed to one pound of pork, growing at 0.759 kilos per day each (far in excess of big

Hamish's record daily liveweight gain), and the fact that we had no deaths earned us a bonus of 30 pence a pig.

So I've £850 for my ten weeks labour and 75 bales of straw. I suppose it is "better than a slap across the belly wi a caul fish", as my father used to say in his courser moments, but it isn't much. We haven't cracked the cash flow problem yet.

Nevertheless being back in pigs has raised my standing in certain quarters and that is always welcome. In fact The Red Rooster was saying that I would now qualify for the sponsored trip to next year's pig fair.

But from what I hear of this year's event that could be something of an assault course. Certainly Mossie was still scouring almost a week after he got home.

There had been such enthusiasm for the pig that one landlord had tried to get "an undisclosed four-figure sum" out of the Scottish delegation by way of compensation. The claim had been met with some good natured unenthusiasm at breakfast when Mossie had suggested that the breakages could be claimed as storm damage. The landlord was furious. "Storm damage?" he had raged, "it's all internal. There's not even a broken window."

"Oh, but we'll soon brak a window for you," said Mossie, helpfully.

69

Cunning device for bulls

WHEN I was in pedigree cattle, I always made a big issue of whether my bulls could walk well. That may not matter too much for the elite among bulls who work in artificial insemination stations but, for the bull which does the business on the hill, movement is vital. If he hasn't got good legs he wont be able to climb the hill let alone do anything when he gets there.

I soon learned how to get the bulls fine and fat. That could be achieved by putting them in a pen with plenty of food. But a lot of food was hard to combine with good movement. Indeed, I found that by the time it came to the bull sales my Charolais looked a picture as long as they stood still. When they walked they looked as though their legs were encased in stucco.

Our answer, as with most pedigree breeders, was long walks with the bulls on halter or tied on behind the tractor, but that was a dreadfully time-consuming business and a better way had to be found.

It was my friend James Jeffrey of Kersknowe who gave me the best idea. In the same way that Gala Fairydean and Rangers are rivals, so it was with the Ardo and Kersknowe herds, but I had noticed that despite James' Charolais being just as fat as mine they flowed easily along beside my staccato offerings.

Now, the first thing a bull does after it has eaten is to drink. And James told me that the Kersknowe bulls were forced to keep themselves active by the cunning device of having the bulls' only source of water half a mile away from their food trough. So, if the bulls are fed four times a day, that's four miles they have to walk.

I tried it and it works well. And what a lot of time it saves.

I was reminded of the Kersknowe bulls the other day as I stumbled along the Howe – the little valley that runs for a mile along the western march of Little Ardo – looking for calving cows. There is no other way of seeing all the cows in the Howe than walking it's length and I try to remember to do that twice a day.

I could of course calve them in the little calfie's park in front of the house but, like the Kersknowe bulls, I need the exercise.

And the need is great, for an interesting situation has arisen in the farmers' discussion group that meets in the Salmon Inn on a Sunday evening.

You will recall that one of the stars is Big Hamish, who has a dairy, a huge tractor and is thinking of selling his £27,000 digger for something better. In addition to that Hamish has an extraordinary ability to thrive. So much so that we could never find out just how big Big Hamish really was. He tramped any domestic scales right round and when he did sneak onto the weighbridge at Maud market we didn't have a witness there and the big man wouldn't tell us… not even in kilos.

Anyway, disaster has hit the farming industry again. At a time when we are in dire need of new markets, one considerable outlet has all-but closed down. Big Hamish has joined Weightwatchers. There are to be no more half-dozens of pies consumed at the mid-morning break and no more boxes of Yorkie Bars in the cab of the digger.

71

It may be bad for trade but the diet is fairly working. Indeed Hamish and the wife have taken off a hundredweight between them. We used to think Mossie with his barley-growing would be the first of the discussion group to make the *Guinness Book of Records* but now it looks like the Pairs Slimming title may be ours before long.

There are two interesting consequences of the shrinking of the big man and neither of them is all good.

The first is that it seems to have given him an enhanced appetite for whisky. At the discussion group last Sunday the nips were disappearing at a quite alarming rate. This, Big Hamish puts down to the amount of slack skin he now has to fill.

And the second is that Hamish and I are now jointly the heaviest in the discussion group. As my weight has edged gently upward it has met Hamish's bulk on the slide.

So you see I need my twice daily walks along the Howe looking for calving cows.

And it looks as though I'll be able to continue my walks for ages. One half of my trans-planted Jerseys produced their calves bang on time but all has been quiet since. The rest appear to have resorbed their embryos and, if so, I'll have weeks more midwifery as we get the dividend from our sweeping bull.

Indeed it looks as though my experiment with the Jersey cows is coming to it's entirely predictable conclusion. The idea was sound. The mothering abilities of the Jerseys can be harnessed to beef production by transplanting beef embryos into them. The progeny do very well and have no narrow Jersey-style rear ends.

But it just doesn't work often enough with the level of neglect operated at Little Ardo. Then there is the problem of what to do with the sweepings because they do have Jersey blood and there just isn't a grade for that sort of beef.

Then again, there's the rate of attrition. Our thirty Jerseys are down to eighteen in two years and even if you count off the five which were non-breeders it does look as though my little Channel Islanders are hardly fit to be hill cows competing with Simmentals and Black Herefords.

Worrying time with awol calf

SOMETIMES MY farming life is purest joy.

My daily walks along the Howe in search of calving cows, for example, can be sheer magic. If I can make it far enough before six I find the cows are still sitting peacefully in that picture of contentment which in humans would be sleep, but in the cows is a sort of seated dwam. I like to see them rise and look around for their calves – and summon them with a gentle maternal lowing to break their fast on udders which, at this time of year, are full to running out first thing in the morning.

And my cows can be fairly aggressive in their maternalism. If the calf is slow, the gentle lowing soon rises to a strident bellow. That brings them and soon they are pulling away, the slavers bubbling down from jaw to grass as the good beast gets on with the job of collecting the grass for the next milking.

The partridges are paired and the pheasants are mating, the hares are back in the best numbers for many years, and our first ever Mistle Thrush is about to launch her four young on the wide world beyond the beech hedge in the garden. All this I see in my early morning walks along with the eager menace of the fox. And it is accompanied by that ageless symphony, the dawn chorus. The wood pigeons provide the steady rhythm section behind the strings of the finches, the brass of the peesies and the curlews, and the woodwind of the blackbirds and the thrushes. We've even got a woodpecker this year. His percussion has been a particular blessing this spring.

Yes, my farming life is often great.

But sometimes it isn't.

We had a Jersey cow calved in the little field in front of our house. A fine bull calf, he was nowhere near able to keep up with the milk supply so we decided to take him and his mother in to give her a second calf to relieve the pressure on her hefted udder.

The prospect of taking in a two-day-old calf and his mother was hardly a daunting one, so we were mildly surprised when the calf set off and led the cows in a couple of laps of the field. The Wasting Asset and I decided to get the cow in and then to return for the calf at leisure.

A backward glance as we left the field showed the calf carefully picking his way through the fence into a field of oil seed rape. We had a bit of a look for him when we had penned the cow, but could find not a trace. Knowing how cows can bellow, and how calves can recognise their mother's roarings, we were confident that the calf would be waiting at the pen in the morning.

Nevertheless I went into the rape field late that night to listen for a ravenous calf. None was to be heard. Despite the confidence I expressed, I started to worry.

Having done so all night, I was up at four thirty determined to hear the calf's first bleat for its morning milk. Up and down the tramlines I went, looking and listening. Nothing was to be heard. Clearly the calf was weak through lack of milk and would be lying down among the rape. For some reason the cow wasn't roaring, so there was nothing to get it going. We were clearly going to have to look for the calf. It just wasn't going to find it's own way home.

If you have looked for a calf in a grass field and eventually found it behind a thistle or a wee tuft of grass, you will appreciate the problem of finding one in 27 acres of rape.

My first move was to run up and down all the tram lines with a tractor. Nothing.

Then the Wasting Asset and I walked the whole field – three passes to the 40 foot tramline. Nothing. I got my neighbours Millie and Mountie Joe to come and comb the fields with their dogs. Joe even offered to bring over his stallion. He thought that the extra height of being on top of the horse would enable him to see the calf. Even if it would likely be dead by now, at least we would know and it would save harvest being spoiled by a grim discovery.

I didn't fancy the horse tramping down my rape anyway, but when a helicopter taking the lads out to the rigs on the North Sea passed, I waved to it in the pathetic hope that they would spare a while for the search.

It was becoming clear that the calf had really taken off. I was sickened by the thought of it bawling in vain round some foreign field before proceeding with its slow death. I toured the countryside, confessed to all my neighbours that I couldn't keep track of my stock, but no-one had seen it. Millie said it could live two days. Mountie Joe said it had been stolen. Hillie said a fox had got it, and Mossie said it was bound to be dead. What a comfort neighbours can be.

After an 18-hour day of searching, I went to bed feeling sick of stomach.

When sleep came it was well into the small hours. But it didn't last long. I was awakened by a tremendous commotion in the field in front of the house. The wanderer had returned and was furious to find that his mother wasn't waiting up for him. He had clearly slept peacefully in the rape for the 36 hours and was hungry at last.

It gets right up my nose

SUMMER is well on its way again. I know that, because the first of the rhubarb that luxuriates in the garden has already been gathered, stewed, left to go mouldy in the refrigerator, and been thrown out. It is one of the less welcome, but more reliable harbingers of summer on this hill.

The grass has started to grow in earnest and is beginning to catch up with the cattle's appetites, the gaps in the oilseed crops are beginning to close as the flowers emerge, and the grain is starting to flatter and perhaps to deceive.

The little thrushes have flown from the beech hedge, and no doubt some of them have already been eaten by cats. Such is nature's sad beauty.

I was pleased to see another of her wonders in the perennial rape park on Friday. As I swept down to the bank to enjoy one last visit before the overdraft was re-established, I saw a flash of brown among the emerging yellow flowers.

My first reaction was that it would be my crops consultant, who has taken quite an interest in the perennial rape field – as it is his first too. I quickly realised though that it was too far from the gate to be the consultant. I looked again and, sure enough, it was a roe deer. I like to think of the rape giving cover to such visitors.

A much less picturesque visitor this week was the young man who comes with his computer to tell me what sort of a mess I am making. As he has to rely on my unreliable bookkeeping for the little he knows, I don't place too much credence on what he says, but here in outline is his diagnosis:

If I don't pay myself any wages, I am making about 1 per cent return on the market value of the assets I employ at Little Ardo. The grain is giving me a little more than set-aside and, believe it or not (I don't), the cattle are paying for the Armstrong (the casual labour I hire from the Buchan Machinery Ring) and leaving me over £100 an acre for the grass. The pigs are giving me £60 a week for seven bales of straw.

If all this be true then surely I am rich?

Not so. Apparently, I am just too big an overhead for 250 acres. The farm that enabled my father to lead the life of a gentleman with inexpensive more work. That is diversifying my farming, and I'm quite happy about that. My neighbour, Hillie, has a snail ranch – and that's diversification. Our farms have a more diverse product mix now.

But what gets right up my nose is when people lecture farmers about how they will need to diversify into pony rides, mountain bike tracks,

vices, as well as a living for six men, cannot give me respectable figures though I have higher yields, and more cows and pigs forbye.

And my accountant's solution? Diversification. And that's a thing that is quite capable of driving me to hysteria.

He's already encouraged me to take on the pigs, and that is alright by me even if it is a bit golf courses, and Bed and Breakfast. I think it is a sad day for the industry, without which we must surely all die, when the advice is pouring in on us from all sides that we should do that sort of diversifying. Turning your farm into a leisure park is not diversifying the industry – it is leaving the industry.

At the discussion group this week we were having a go at

77

that topic, and it was the Red Rooster who came up with a novel 'diversification'. He is untramelled by wives and children and yet lives in one of those Victorian houses built in the golden age of agriculture when to be a tenant of a three pair place on the estate of the Earls of Aberdeen was a measure of substance.

Now, the Rooster has come across a firm of fly-men from Aberdeen who act for the city's oil companies. This man has offered the Rooster £1000 a month for the rent of his farmhouse.

Of course, the lads were appalled by the thought of one of the most efficient of the North-East's grain barons diversifying into a caravan in his close.

"Dinna worry about me, boys," said the Rooster. "Wi' my thousand pounds a month I'll be living in the Mercury Motor Inn."

The discussion group had to be conducted at a higher pitch this week due to an invasion of the Salmon Inn by a hoard of thirsty young farmers from Bute.

They were up in the North-East on a cultural and educational exchange. Certainly they seemed to have learned of quite a few watering holes of which I hadn't heard, but they had little to say of what they had learned of agricultural interest. They seemed a nice bunch, despite the noise, and they were good enough to invite me down to Bute for the return leg of the cultural exchange.

I believe that it would be fun, and that they could expand my mind but, having seen them on Sunday night and on Monday morning, I really think I am too old.

One back for my friendly phonecalls

MY HEART sank when the phone rang on Thursday evening at half past eight. It had been a hard day and a long one and there was something about the way it rang that told me that it was a call-out.

I have forty-seven neighbours here and they are very good about phoning me up to tell me that my cattle are needing attention. Sometimes they are right and sometimes it is even something that can be sorted. It can save me losses and then I am grateful.

But while my neighbours here are kind and generous in their concern for the welfare of my animals, only eight of them are farmers and not all of them know much about livestock. So I get a lot of calls.

There is a little field down by the river and just across from the ten houses which form the bit of our village called Blackcraig. Sure as death if I have a calf born in that field the phone will start to ring. "Hallo, Charlie. Is that you? I dinna like the look of yon calfie. He's aye sleeping", was one this Spring. That calf had to do a lot of sleeping to try to deal with the five gallons of milk it's mother was providing for it.

And "I dinna think that calfie's sookin", was another warning. Of course the calf was never seen sucking because it only needed two bellyfuls a day and it took it's first at five in the morning. When I went to check it that calf was as round as a hogshead of wine.

I even had a phone call from a policewoman last Spring to say that my best Simmental cow was lying dead in that park. Despite the false alarms of the past, that call fairly spoiled my tea. It is easy for the inexperienced to make mistakes but this girl was a vet's daughter and death is a fairly emphatic condition.

I excused myself from our guests, grabbed a hosepipe in case she had blown up and might yet be saved and raced down to the field by the river.

All was peaceful. There wasn't even one beast sitting down. My cow was grazing and the picture of health.

But of course, you never know. It could be serious so I always act on my friendly phone-calls. It was with resignation that I answered on Thursday evening. But any lethargy was soon dispelled.

"That big Simmental coo is far from well. She's showdin' about all over the place and has fallen doon twice an slaverin' hellish. She's gaun tae tak' staggers."

You might think that was nothing to worry about in the light of the other calls I've told you about, but this was from the man who looks after the Red Rooster's hill cows. He lives in one of the houses that overlooks the Waterside park.

We really don't get staggers these days because we give the cows ad-lib magnesium syrup. But this cow might well be short of magnesium as she was one of four that I had bought at Thainstone Mart that day. They'd been part of a large consignment of cows with Belgian Blue calves at foot and they had been badly cared for. They were thin, dirty and looked in need of worming.

Just how rough they were can be gauged by the fact that in a sale which saw twelve hundred topped and many bids above a thousand, those four cows with bull calves at foot averaged four hundred and ninety pounds.

So staggers was definitely on.

I got her a feed of barley soused in Magnesium syrup and hurried down to the waterside.

There was no doubt she was in a bad way. A great big lump of a cow she was indeed staggering all over the place and frothing at the mouth. I tried her with my bucket but she was not for it. She was shivering and a pathetic spectacle. I thought I knew what was needed... to put a rope on her and get a bottle of magnesium into her.

But staggers is a nervous disease as well as a deficiency and I feared that the very act of roping her would bring on the fit which would likely kill her and certainly leave her down.

Against my ingrained prejudices I called the vet.

He came and roped her. The poor thing fell down, but not in a fit. She was just dizzy with fever. The intravenous bottle, not of magnesium but of calcium, was administered.

My new cow had milk fever.

"A good sign that," I thought. "It shows that when faced with starvation she is putting the little available calcium into milk for the calf. She'll be a good mother when we feed her."

Within a minute she was looking calmer and brighter of eye. In half an hour she was grazing.

That's one back for the vets. And one back for my friendly farming phone-callers.

Cash for weeds not cricket

YOU FIND the farmer bewildered. He has just read in the *Sunday Telegraph* that a new setaside scheme is to be brought in which will offer £160 an acre to farmers if they reduce their sowings by 100 per cent. In 1945 my father paid £19 an acre and for that he got the title deeds. In the early 1970s I added another twenty acres to the place for £105 an acre and there was a house and a very antiquated steading in the deal.

And now I am offered £160 an acre just to grow weeds?

The discussion group that meets in the Salmon Inn was in some excitement at this as you can imagine. No one would believe me at first but when I produced the paper they began to take the whole thing very seriously indeed.

The Red Rooster, who has already decided to move out to the Mercury Motor Inn and rent the farmhouse to an oilman for £1000 a month, now sees the prospects of a gross margin of £160 for taking just two cuts at the weeds per year.

Mossie the great cerealiser, was really scared by the prospect. A great vista of available

time opened up before his eyes. His seven hundred acres at £160 was easy to count at £100,000 a year even after paying his man to cut the stuff. Better still, he could sack the man, let out the house and cut the weeds himself.

But Mossie hasn't gained his reputation as the Guru of the discussion group without merit as a thinker. I asked why he had blanched. "I'm just thinkin' aboot my liver", he said. "If I go for setaside I'll just have too much free time."

On the other hand Big Hamish who is a bit nervous in such discussions as he isn't sure how much a per cent is, is all for the scheme. "Well boys, you can say what you like, I'm going to gie them a hunder per cent and maybe mair if it's a success". Hamish's idea is that he'll go a hundred and fifty per cent setaside and spend his time contracting. He hasn't seen that if half of Aberdeenshire is in setaside there'll be a slack demand for contractors.

What about the farmer of this fine two pair place? Is my tenure of this hill to be remembered as the time when the toil of my forefathers was overthrown for a mess of weeds? What would William Yull think of his great great grandson? What would John Yull think? What would Maitland Mackie think of the grandson he took round his many farms during the war, if he looked down and saw the weeds growing on the fields he had passed onto that side of the family?

And what would my father think? Alone among my ancestors he might understand but I shudder to think of how John R. Allan, as a master wordsmith, might have expressed his sorrow.

Anyway, Mossie has thought the thing through and I, who can't be bothered to think it through, am going with him. If hundred per cent setaside at £160 an acre comes in we're going to soldier on. According to Mossie we'll make a fortune (again, in his case). So much of the Scottish cereal acreage will disappear that there will be a desperate shortage of cereals to feed the livestock. Better than that, this stock-rearing area will be acutely short of straw and we'll be able to get ten pound a bale for that... another hundred pounds an acre at least.

Frankly, I hate setaside. And I hate it in the way that I hate 'diversification' of the type that is not diversification of farming but it's abandonment in favour of some other activity. They will have the cheek to say that setaside is part of the cost of supporting agriculture when it is nothing of the kind. Paying good men and true to grow weeds does not support farming. That ends farming.

Only the ignorant and the Philistine could call growing weeds farming. Farming might be defined as growing anything but weeds.

And I fear not only for my farm but for my countryside if this madness succeeds. For I have seen what happens when a farming tradition is overturned by diversification and by setaside.

There is a part of the Island of Rhodes which has grown food and wine for thousands of years but which will be forever barren. The men have taken setaside in return for ripping out their vines. They have used the money to go in for tourism. The terraces which were there before Christ are damaged beyond repair and in a few short years the skills that once made them productive have gone.

May that not happen in Buchan.

Jerseys eat more daintily

I SEE that Reading University is taking up my idea of transplanting pure beef embryos into Jersey cows. They are not readers of the *Glasgow Herald*, I fear, for they seem very pleased about the originality of their idea to get the mothering ability of the Jersey without having to suffer the pointed rear end which Jersey crosses tend to produce.

The boffins have done a computer simulation of the herds performance and that shows that the idea is sound and that it will leave £926 per hectare. It may well... but I must warn them that it is a lot easier to farm on a computer than it is on a farm.

With the hindsight that my many disasters have given me, I advise against buying the cheapest old bangers at displenishing sales. There is no doubt your chances are much better with fresh young cows.

Don't run the Jerseys with a mixture of pure Simmentals and Hereford-Friesians. The poor wee Channel Islanders just aren't tough enough. I found that if I was to keep the condition on the Jerseys I had to feed the black and whites more than was necessary and the Simmentals got positively fat. That must be because the Jerseys eat more daintily... pinkies -up like my granny's bridge ladies. I'm sure they would be economical if fed alone.

It is vital to keep the condition on the recipients or they may lose their calves. This year half the calves diagnosed at six weeks didn't materialise. There was no sign of abortion so I presume they were resorbed.

Be good to your Jerseys for they can lose heart. We had two this year which just gave up.

One was poor little Lottie the one with the twisted face who could eat round corners. We found her stuck at the calving one morning. The calf came out easily enough but Lottie was partly paralysed in her back legs. That usually passes after a day or two and, as we had her up on her feet that day, we expected all to be well.

But Lottie had just had enough. Though we hoisted her up twice a day, and though she could support herself easily, she just refused to eat. A fortnight later she was dead. I went down first thing to try to tempt her with some grass soaked in treacle. She was sitting normally in the sleeping position, but she didn't respond to my call. Another job for the digger.

It was Lottie's death that made me change my policy. I just don't have the time nor the facilities to give the Jerseys the individual treatment they need. The Simmentals are my first love and the Hereford Friesians are doing well so it is the Jerseys which have to go.

Fortunately they are finding a ready market among the white settlers.

I have bought 30 Black Hereford heifers from Somerset for £65 each. They're off the milk now and looking well though they are a bit away from their first calving. In the meantime I'm keeping up my numbers by buying in cross cows from the bottom end of the market... the end I know best.

I mustn't be too hard on the Jerseys. The transplant calves this year could hardly be bettered. Last year's were too dumpy but my new calves are excellent. If Reading University get calves like mine they may yet do as well as the computer.

All my troubles haven't been with the Jerseys. I had a Simmental heifer calved six weeks early. The calf lived for a day. Big Hamish came to the rescue with a Simmental cross Friesian heifer calf but I would have to go for it.

The farm car being on scarecrow duty and stuck in the mud I only had the Sunday car. I've never been too sure of the legality of carrying calves in the boot though they never seem to mind, but I was a bit nervous especially as I had no bag and the wife would kill me if she thought I was using the good car.

I shut the heifer in and set off for home with a nervous eye for white cars. I had every reason to worry. My car is a hatchback and the boot is not the secure place it looks. As I was speeding through New Deer the flimsy cardboard cover burst as the calf got to his feet. He spent the rest of the trip looking out of the back window.

I was looking out too... for the police... but I didn't see any... and they didn't see me.

Shotgun put end to game

FROM THE plump hand of Angus there runs North through the county of Kincardineshire a thin finger of prosperity that points mockingly at the thin lands of my forefathers here in Aberdeenshire. I refer of course to the Howe of the Mearns. This is surely God's first agricultural gift. Here even a bad farmer can expect to grow three tonnes of malting barley and lift twenty tonnes of potatoes.

In the hard times between the wars my grandfather, the original Maitland Mackie, was able to buy the best farm in the Mearns for £19,000, a fact which has made an uncle and a cousin of mine very happy ever since.

The cheek of a tenant farmer in Aberdeenshire having The Bent as an out-farm brought the old man into contact with a different type of farmer. The wealthy farmers of the Mearns had time for eccentricity.

Chief among those was John Robertson of the fine farm of Drumnagair. Old Drumlie wasn't everyone's cup of tea and some of the stories told about him should not be told of the dead, but he had a quite unusual capacity for life. To old Drumlie moderation seems to have been little more than wasted opportunity.

He had music in him. His son arrived late at Montrose feein' market one year and joined a huge crowd cranning to see a music-based street entertainment. This turned out to be old Drumlie dancing a stately gavotte to the music of a tink wife's tin whistle. Poor Wull was then too young to see the beauty of the scene and saw only the shame.

Yes old Drumlie had music in him and romance too. He had fancied the job of engine-driver as a lad so when the time came to go to Smithfield in the train he insisted on riding up front where he helped with the stoking of the boiler and kept the driver, the fireman and himself well stoked with whisky all the way to London.

Then there was the run-in he had with the footballers.

Drumlie and a crony arrived home after a day's serious drinking at the Mart to find that young Wull had allowed the cotter loons to play football in the wee park beside the house. The six young stegs (Clydesdale colts) were enjoying the game too, charging around in a state of high excitement.

Fou though they were, the two farmers could see that this wasn't in the horseman's masterplan.

"By God Drumlie, I widna let thae bairns upset the stegs like that."

"No, by God, Mains, and neither would I," said Drumlie and disappeared into the house. He appeared moments later with the shotgun and gave the ball both barrels.

That fairly stopped the game.

Now, you might think that was an extreme action to take and even Drumlie, that man of extremes, seems to have agreed. For next day he yoked the gig and drove the thirty-five miles into Aberdeen from which he returned that evening with a brand new football.

Meanwhile on the thin lands of Aberdeenshire the loons couldn't afford footballs and the farmers couldn't afford to shoot and replace them. The loons on Little Ardo were subject to a more elemental and a more predictable discipline.

That was administered for forty-six years by the great Jimmy Low, grieve to my grandfather whom he revered as a great farmer and teacher, to my father whom he cherished as a friend and as a writer, and latterly to me, whom he regarded with the affection due to a soft-headed son and the contempt due to a farmer who did things differently.

The loons went in awe of Auld Low, as he was known from the age of twenty-five. It was usually unnecessary for him to do anything for we were all touched by his quiet menace. But if he did have to act it was with such ferocity that it lasted a long time.

Take the case of Colin Dickie, the dairy cattleman's second boy. There was no devilment up to which Colin could not rise. For a while it seemed that Auld Low had met his match. That was until the great day when he went round to the back of the tattie shed and caught Colin delivering the stone that brought his total of broken window panes to thirty seven… for the day, that is.

Now there stands in the wood at Little Ardo an old milk house which has been used so long to keep coal that it is the blackest place this side of hell. Auld Jimmy caught the culprit and took him gently but firmly to the coalshed. He put the lad in and waited till the whimper-ing started to rise. "Now Colin, if I ever catch you at the fairm again I'll put you in there and I'll never let you oot."

I don't know what the educational psychologists would say about that but as a system of man-management it was effective. I expect Colin did just as much damage but he did it elsewhere and that wasn't Auld Jimmy's concern.

Lost on the way to Ingliston

HIGHLAND SHOW time again and that means the culmination of weeks of careful planning. And not just by the stocksmen and women who have laboured to make fair beasts look like good ones and good beasts look great. The boys that meet at the Salmon Inn on a Sunday have been hard at the planning too.

For many the logistics of the Highland Show are little more than a well worn path. They have been so often before that they know where they want to stay, what time to arrive to see the best of everything, what time to leave before the police get too active around the Forth Road Bridge and so on. But it is not so simple for the Red Rooster, Crookie and Mossie... the Grain Barons of Buchan. They tend to have to choose their hotel by a process of elimination... they start by eliminating all the hotels they have stayed in previously.

"They must be ill to please", I hear you say, but that is not the point... it is the hoteliers who seem to be too narrow-minded.

They had a good example at the Pig Fair at the Royal Showground this year. There had been a very nice party at their hotel in Coventry. The boys had been in a jolly mood and all seemed to be going well. The pleasant atmosphere was quite spoiled at breakfast though, when the landlord presented the lads with a bill which would have bought a good bull at Perth.

Having no recollection of any mishaps the guests were unimpressed and Mossie told the manager that he should claim any breakages off his insurance. "Put it in as storm damage," he suggested, helpfully.

That seemed to upset the manager who turned redishy-purple. "Storm damage?" he said, "But there's not even a broken window".

"Oh, but we'll soon break a window for you", said Mossie,

even more helpfully.

With experience like that you can see that the choice of hotel for the Highland was an important one. Mossie was aghast to find that only one hotel had been booked for the three nights. The normal precaution of getting a different hotel each night had been overlooked. What were they to do on the second and third nights?

Mossie decided that there would have to be a change. "Right boys this year we'll have a working day for a start." I, who regard all my days at the Highland as hard work, wanted to know what the difference between a working day and a normal day was to be.

After some hesitation; "On the workin' day we winna drink so much".

You'd think a man with so much regard for machinery and so little regard for profit as Big Hamish would be going to the show for sure, but he's not, and that despite winning four days there free. That was in a competition run all over the North East for the man who could spot the most faults in a Case International tractor.

In my entry I tried them with "It's too dear" but it was explained that it was deliberate faults only that were allowed. I couldn't see how they could claim that the price wasn't deliberate, but I did know what they meant.

Well Hamish had no difficulty in spotting all ten faults. The weight frame was upside down, one wheel was set wider than the other, the check chains were wrongly set, the indicator glass was back-to-front. The only thing I managed was the number-plate being upside down so I was impressed by Hamish's win.

But he wasn't impressed by the four days at the Highland and plumped instead for the second prize of a week's free use of a new, 120 horsepower tractor. It's come in handy for the silage-making and for taking down to the village for several errands a day in case anyone hasn't seen his new £30,000 toy.

But the rest of us will all be there again, though I must say the show has lost some of its excitement, since it settled down at Ingliston. You know that each year the judging rings will be on the North side of the arena. The breed society stands will overlook the judging rings and that appalling factory for expensive headaches (the Herdsman's Bar) will be as raucous and rank as ever.

Things were, of course, al-

together worse in the grand old days when the Highland went to a different part of the country each year, but at least it was unpredictable. It last came to Aberdeen in 1959 and that was unpredictable for you.

It rained constantly and the showground at Hazlehead rapidly turned into a quagmire and then a lake. Some of the Shorthorns and Blacks which were bred, in the words of the late Bob Adam, "as low to the ground as possible" were scraping their undercarriages on the judging ponds, polite ladies from 'the toon' abandoned their shoes and went barefoot, the man who was selling umbrellas and wellingtons ran out of stock six times and the *Press and Journal* carried a picture of a farmer who had walked out of a wellington looking longingly back at it stuck firmly in the mud.

There'll be no such fun at Ingliston this time. The permanent site has tarmac roadies all round it so the weather can do it's worst... even in most of the car parks.

That's all to the good, of course, but something has been lost. When the Show came to your area everybody went. That meant it covered a wider audience over the years and that it had a Dumfries feel about it one year and an Inverness feel the next. There was more of an air of the unexpected. Now the same people go each year and we all know what to expect.

Mind you the committee have made a stout effort this year to give us something new and potentially of considerable benefit to our beleaguered industry. The entire ground floor of the exhibition centre is being given over to Food from Scotland which, in the words of immediate past Chairman Robin Forrest, provides a "platform for all sections of the Scottish food industry' to show off their wares. "After all, when you go to the Paris Show they show you French food". There had been the Food Fair of course but, while that had been a great innovation in it's time it had ceased to sparkle; it had not been Scottish and it had not been on anything like this year's scale.

Five hundred potential buyers of our farm produce are to be dined by the Royal Highland and Agricultural Society and it is hoped they'll buy plenty. The do is to be hosted by Sir David Nixon of Scottish Enterprise. The Scottish Quality Beef and Lamb Association and the Bowmore Distillery are the principal sponsors and more important visitors than me include the Princess Royal, The Minister of Agriculture, The Secretary of State for Scotland and Lord Strathclyde.

It's a really worthy effort and quite unlike what one might expect from anything with a name so like Food from Britain... that was all mouth and no movement.

Farmers facing a taxing time

THERE IS no doubt we are ruined again. It is uncanny how, just when it begins to seem as though we are going to survive after all, authority slams the boot in once more.

And it really was beginning to look as though we were to be spared for at least a little longer. The price review (as it is no longer called) was far less worse than we had been expecting. After all the talk there has been of putting a stop to the excesses of the Common Agricultural Policy, of throwing us onto a world market for food, their proposals for this year are not so very bad. At a time when the captains of British industry are having to make do with salary increases of up to 43 per cent farmers are to be let off with price cuts of only a few per cent... maybe ten per cent after inflation.

And boys like us can easily stand that sort of dunt. At least we will if we're clever enough at the farming. And the funny thing is that everything is really not looking too bad here. The wheat is certainly looking better than last year despite the cold weather and so is the winter barley. The rape is hardly doing as well but then last year's thirty-one hundredweight crops were never likely to be repeated.

Mind you of my five fields of winter rape three are looking first rate. The perennial park (the one I didn't sow but simply left the aftermath) looks remarkably well. It could even be average yet. And even the park from which the seeds all blew away last September is looking better. Despite having no more than one plant to the square metre it has filled in and you'd hardly notice it from the road. It is no longer a disgrace... just a disaster.

The pigs are proving to be a joy. Now that we are fully automatic they are really no work at all. We'd had the latest batch of two hundred for twenty-two days before I had to do anything. I love to sneak down to the piggery and listen. Every few minutes there is a gentle swish for a few seconds and I know that they have been fed again. What a change to the dreadful corners round which the barrowfuls of wet meal had to rowed in my grandfather's time.

And then I have still got fourteen fine bulls to sell and at this time last year I had nothing to look forward to but the grazers and harvest.

So you see the job was working better than sometimes before they hit us with this.

I refer to the witch-hunt that we are being subjected to over the licensing of farm vehicles. This has always been an optional tax and it is one out of which the farmers of Aberdeenshire have usually opted.

We have always believed that it was OK for a farmer to drive on the road as long as he wasn't caught, that the police weren't very much bothered until you hit someone, and that even then you were allowed a few miles a week on the roads without a licence. It seems to me that over the years the number alleged to be allowed has risen and stands at thirteen miles. This means you could drive grain to a store thirteen miles away and tell the bobbies

that you weren't coming back, or, if they stopped you on the way back, you could say the tractor had been there for a week on loan.

Well we know better now and we have Mossie to thank for that.

He is, of course, a Grain Baron with the best part of a thousand acres of crop and as such has men and lots of machinery on which to put licences but, like the rest of us, he had been economising. He happened on one of his tractors which had been stopped by a squad car.

"Well, what's your excuse?" said the genial policemen. And when he saw Mossie's puzzled expression, "Well you fairmers usually have a story."

If it was a story the policemen wanted they had certainly come to the right man... but they had come prepared.

"Oh the licence. Aye it's at home."

"No, it canna' be. We've a print-out of all the licensed vehicles and yours is not on it."

Nice try Mossie but not good enough. "Oh it must be that wife of mine nae payin' attention. I'll need to speak to her. But surely a farmer is allowed thirteen miles without a

licence?"

"No its only six miles in the week" said the patient officer who had seen a farmer squirming on that hook before.

"But he's only gone six miles", said Mossie getting desperate.

"Well now, that's funny. For we've followed him for eight miles and he disna' seem to be hame yet."

Mossie could see he was beat.

"How much is that going to cost me?" he asked.

And that was the good news. You only get fined half the cost of the licence, currently fifteen pounds. Mossie said it was good value after all the years and all the vehicles and all the miles they had done without a licence.

It was like the flockmaster who long ago summered his sheep on the 'lang park' as we call the roadside. There had been a drought on and he'd kept his two hundred lambs going on the roads for three weeks before the bobbies had put a stop to it. The judge had told our man about the dangers of having flocks of sheep always on the road with all these cars there were nowadays and how he was lucky there hadn't been an accident.

The shepherd was fined three pounds whereupon he asked the court if he could have the grazing next year at the same price.

But despite the fact that a fine of half the cost seems like a bargain we are all rushing to get everything legal. The Post Office at Ellon has long queues. I've two tractors and a digger to licence. Mossie has done all his tractors, loaders and combines. The Red Rooster was a bit snooty because he always had licenses but the rush to legality has even hit Potions the chemist who has decided to licence his ride-on mower with which he keeps our roadsides tidy.

We don't mind much but it is just another overhead we could well have continued to do without.

Stallion's honour satisfied

THE HIGHLIGHT of the Royal Highland Show, as far as I was concerned, was my chance meeting with an old friend. I had had a jolly liquid lunch with my unrelated uncle, Willie Allan the Galloway, Simmental and Snail Breeder from Glenturk. He told me he has left the glen and moved north to Perthshire. That seemed to me to be altogether a civilising move though perhaps it still had a bit to go. At any rate Willie's son Brian, who now has the running of the place unhindered by his father's advice, seemed particularly happy about the move.

I was keen to make contact with another old pal to see if I could jog his memory about the fifty pounds I had lent him last year and had been told that he had been seen taking up more than his fair share of the Sheep Breeders Association tent. Unfortunately, I arrived just after Bert had been rolled out of the bar. Looking casually round for friendly faces I lit upon Ian Skea.

We had sung together, played together and been caught together at the university about the time when the fifties were becoming the sixties. Since then he had been an itinerant farm manager, mostly for the Overseas Development Administration. He had introduced ovine Blackfaces to the high Andes, grown sugar in the South Seas and he had kept the biggest and best herd of dual purpose goats in Kenya. No wonder then that Skea was browner than he used to be and, though he was still not a big man, he was certainly a good deal thicker.

Among his virtues the chiefest is Ian Skea's ability to tell the old tales and to make up new ones. And I was delighted to find him in that element. He had cornered a young victim who was polite enough to be listening intently. When I joined them there were two of us raking over all the things that had happened so long ago and been through so many hands that they were quite untrammelled by truth.

The young man made an excuse and left us. "Making good his escape," thought I. Wrong again. He appeared moments later with three large ones. He was obviously enjoying himself. I like to think of the day thirty years from now when that young man collars the latest young man and tells him about the garrulous old men who used to tell stories at the Highland Show way back in the nineties. That's heritage for you.

I can't tell you all Skea's stories, that wouldn't be fair, but I will tell you about the time he showed the stallion at Cunningsburgh Show.

Whenever Skea came to visit his native Northern Isles he tried to relive as much of his youth as possible. He would borrow a dog and try for the prize as the furthest travelled shepherd at the trials. Or he would get a black bullock and show him at the Dounby show.

Well, this visit coincided with the great show of Shetland ponies at Cunningsburgh and Skea would enter. He knew that his old friend John Irvine had a very good stallion down among the dunes at Sumburgh Farm and asked if he could show him.

"Du can show de begger if du can catch him." was John Irvine's reply.

I'll tell you the rest in Ian Skea's own words in that crowded beer tent at Ingliston.

"I got a rope and lay doon on the sand jist like a coyote would do. Shetland stallions are that inquisitive I kent he would come snuffing in aboot to see what this was. Sure enough he came and I got the rope on him but there was nowhere to tie him up. So I dragged him eight miles home... mostly on his back legs. We were nearly home when I got a bit driftwood on the beach and managed to give him a bit of a hiding. After that he was all right. Honour was satisfied. He'd resisted well and got a hiding for it and there was no sense in getting another. But some Americans had seen this wild man chastising a pony on the beach and reported to their landlady that they didn't know that Shetlanders mistreated their horses that way.

"Anyway I got him tied up at the farm, trimmed his tail and off we went to Cunningsburgh Show.

"The judge for the day was a lady from Scotland with bonny tight breeks and quite a lot in them as seems to be quite common wi' that kind o' folk. The first thing she did was to produce this measuring stick and she held it up against each of the thirty four stallions in the class. And my bonnie stallion was just a wee bit too big. So was Willie Irvine's and that meant he was immediately relegated to thirty-third place with me thirty fourth.

"We werena too downhearted and made our way to the bottom of the line where we had recourse to our standard issue half bottles and settled to see how the lady would sort out the winners. But this lady had come a long way and was going to give value for money. She insisted on placing all the stallions right down to Willie and me.

"After maybe half an hour she came down to us and had a look in the mouths. Then she gave me a shift up to thirty-third. About this time the rain came on heavier.

"Now the field at Cunningsburgh is dry enough at the top end, but with a class of thirty-four Willie and me were sinking fast in the green bog at the bottom. 'Come on now with your stick, madam', says Willie. 'I'm sure my stallion's no too big noo.'

"'Well now I believe that other one is even bigger,' said the lady and moved Willie up to thirty-third and me back down to thirty-fourth.

"As the rain came on heavier and I sunk further in the moss the judge came back, lifted Willie's tail, saw something she didn't like and moved me up out of the worst of it and back into thirty-third again. She was back three more times

100

and changed us again and again before she relented and let us back out of the boggy bit and we got away home.

"As we trudged up the hill onto the bit of the field that was only wet I told Willie philo- sophically that somebody had to be last and somebody had to be second last.

"'Och I know, but we've both been both three times each in the one competition.' said Willie."

Mossie's barbecue takes off

I'VE TOLD you before of my outrage at all this talk of how we, in the once proud industry of farming, must diversify. There is too much food so we must diversify. It's not that people have found a way to live without food. The stuff is as vital as ever but we've produced a little too much so we are told that we are to leave the industry by setting aside, starting riding schools or golf courses, or by turning the family home into a hotel. It is such cheek. There is far too much hot air produced and yet no one but me is telling the politicians to diversify.

Having said that I have to report that one of our number has decided to diversify... indeed he has done it. Ever the progressive, Mossie has become an itinerant caterer. You will remember that when his third and unexpectedly-born daughter needed her head wetting, the great man adapted his old muckspreader into a barbecue. That was quite a success

though there was a snag in getting the Power Take Off to run slow enough and the flying fat was reckoned to be a fire hazard. This was overcome by adapting the motor from the side-knife of the combine which turned the spit at just the right speed.

But now, with harvest approaching and the monsoon making sure that the crops are flat enough to give plenty of work for the side knife, Mossie has installed a state-of-the-art motor in the old muckspreader. That means he no longer needs the tractor and can transport the barbecue behind the pick-up. He has even got brake lights, hazards and indicators on it now.

He's in great demand and it's no wonder for it is a good service. Mossie provides the pig, the barbecue, the gas, the chef and a liberal supply of jokes all for £200. I saw him in action at the BASF open day at the Castle of Auchry (their experimental farm just up the road). There he was beaming out of the smoke and smell of a 75 kilo porker, the white chefs hat beginning to wilt and looking less than the full Persil, cutting great dodds of crackling and dumping it on the paper plates. "Come on boys eat her up. If you finish this een I'll get sale for anither een. Oh it's a great way to get rid o' the deed eens...saves time wi' the digger. Come away dear. Never mind yer diet. This is a low cholesterol polyunsaturated pig. Ye ken. Specially selected... I found it mysel." and only pausing to catch breath or to throw another graipful of spare ribs onto the fire.

Of course there isn't always a casualty of a convenient size and then Mossie has to select one from his fattening house. Like the time last week when the Drumfishery Parent Teacher's Association Committee were having their party to finish off the surplus funds at the end of their two years in office. There were only the six of them plus seven wives and sweethearts so Mossie reckoned a fifteen kilo piggy was all that was required... it would be sweeter anyway.

Now, as you will appreciate, you can't very well send an artic to Inverurie with one piggy, so our man just bunged him in on the floor of the pick-up and set off. And that was Mossie's undoing.

For it proved to be a most engaging pig and a very curious one. Soon he had snuffed all round the floor. He'd eaten the few crumbs left in the potato crisp packets and rejected the empty cigarette packets and jumped up onto the seat. There he snuffled round again, had a blow or two at the ashtray, checked out Mossie's jacket pocket and was soon ready for a look at the wider world. He had a squint out of the side window and liked what he saw. He then got his front feet up on the back of the seat and looked eagerly out of the back window. Good though that clearly was, it wasn't enough for this progressive and forward-looking piggy who wanted to see where he was going and soon he had his feet up on the dashboard and was looking eagerly to the left and the right, grunting and snorting little comments to the driver and occasionally checking him out with a wet nose.

Now, in common with most pig farmers, Mossie is not famed for his sentimen-

tality but the irony of this new friendship began to get to him. Especially when they passed a particularly flat field of winter barley when the piggy gave a squeal of what Mossie swore was sheer contempt. And when they got to the slaughterhouse and this particularly large and unpleasant-looking killer advanced upon the pick-up, our man could stand it no longer. He slammed the truck into reverse and raced home to Mossside as fast as was compatible with the safety of his passenger. There he returned the pig to its pen and, shutting his eyes, grabbed another at random. This little piggy went to market in a bag and had no opportunity for spurious friendships.

It was all so different from my little granddaughter who comes to visit us from Edinburgh. She's the product of our elder Wasting Asset and an angel with long blond ringlets and a pouting mouth in which butter would be safe all day. Last time she was shown the pigs her wise question was "Can you eat them?". And now that she is three and a half she went back down to the piggery to see the 199 porkers and said "Are they ready yet?" We were scared to say yes.

She has what it takes to make a farmer.

Silage was a terrible disgrace

WE GOT some sunshine last week and we've been so grateful for it. The crops have grown well with all that water but we were so badly in need of the sun. The grain barons were beginning to make sick jokes about this being another 1987 when everybody north of Perth lost a hundred pounds an acre on their cereals.

But we've had some sun now and the heads are looking fuller.

It was too late for my silage though. That was awful and probably a disgrace. I have heard of silage being made with the bree running out of the backs of the carts but we have never taken it as wet as this year. The weather could hardly have been worse but I really have myself to blame. It is not as though we had a dairy herd and needed to get the highest digestibility silage we possibly could. We could just as well have let it grow on and produce more low-value bulk. But I panicked and made silage soup.

Indeed it was packet soup for we were wrapping the silage individually in big round bales. We used a tubeliner last year but that seemed poor on at least two grounds.

The tubeliner had to work in the field and that meant I was spending about an hour a day all winter running to, and getting stuck in, the field. And then all that running on the grass in winter spoiled about an acre of each silage park. So this year I wanted them home when they were ensiled and left handy beside the sheds.

It hasn't worked out that way though. The plan was to stack the bales three high and that was what we did... a great black stack appeared and spread round the steading. It looked well too, at first. But after a day or two our stack has shrunk to little more than half and our round bales have squashed themselves into soggy triangles. We have what are probably the first big triangular bales in the country. I would patent the idea if I thought there was the slightest chance of the silage being good.

Mossie, infuriating fellow that he is, got his silage in great order. He just left it a couple of weeks and got it during the heatwave. He doesn't use it himself so what does he care about value and, of course, he has two weeks extra growth to sell. No wonder some of my friends from the south were doubting if the man exists and challenged me to produce him at the Highland Show. He was there but, having found that the Pig Improvement Company had the best bar, he hid there for all of the day I had at the show.

Anyway, all is not lost. I dragged one of the triangular bales out of the loch of effluent before sitting down to write this and the fourteen bulls I still have inside are wolfing up at it with no sign of nausea.

Since the silage I have just been doing little tidying-up jobs. I've mended the piggery doors that have been hit by so many tractors that they no longer reached low enough to fit in the grooves made to support them. Both halves used to fly out in a wind and it was only a matter of time before a big gust took them away. Four plates, a lick of paint and they

look as good as fairly old.

With the help of Potions (the local chemist who comes to play) I've painted five of the steading doors and the new second-hand pig-feed bin. That sort of thing does help to cheer the place up and it makes Potions very excited. If he had his way he would have the whole place painted, the broken window panes replaced, the broken gutters fixed and the close swept. I have to restrain him with the wise words I have heard before he was born: "You'll never take the rent out of the close" I tell him.

For that we'll need to get some cattle fat or wait for harvest... events which promise reasonably well.

I particularly look forward to harvest to see how my perennial rape does, and to see the bank coming back into focus.

But I also look forward to harvest as the time when we must win the crop and also best our neighbours. My late father and James Presley, whose farms glower across Ythanvale at one and other, never lost an opportunity to put the other down. Whoever started first would hang about the village in the hope of meeting the other in order to ask "What the hell are you scutterring about at?" And whoever finished first would opine to the other, if he could catch him, that this was no time still to be harvesting.

There was such a rivalry on two farms over at the coast and one side thought to take the lead in the harvest stakes by unveiling in the field a brand new, shiny red grain cart. A four tonner, it was by far the biggest that had been seen in that modest farming country. And as they filled the great cart the tractorman became more and more impressed. They had been filling for ages and still no sign of the cart being full. "By god this is some cairt," he said to himself in wonder and the pride of ownership.

But the neighbours were not bested on that occasion. From the other side of the valley they could see that the cart was never filling because the tail door of the new cart was open. When the combine reached the top of the field, driver and tractorman were able to look back on a trail of golden grain. It's little misfortunes like that, that make the harvest such a fulfilling time... when they befall your neighbours.

Squashed hens made most cash

MY FATHER used to tell me often of an early diversification. It was conceived and executed long before there was a Common Agricultural Policy.

It happened on one of those unfortunate farms where the steading lies at both sides of the road. The farmer kept hens which, as usual, were not paying. It was in the 1930s and prices were on the slide.

The motor car was becoming more and more popular and a growing class of city dwellers were getting into the habit of putting on their tweeds and taking a run into the country to see what the peasants were doing; to find a little country pub for a spot of luncheon. At weekends there would be a veritable stream of cars blazing through the farm yard.

Every now and then, quite often in fact, a hen would be run over by one of those cars. The proud owner would get out to see if there were any scratches on his vehicle and then be shamed into offering compensation for the lost bird.

And the farmer noticed that those that were run over were by far the best payers. A hen in those days would have made maybe two shillings, yet he was never offered less than half a crown, a ten bob note was quite common and he once got a pound for an old hen that was off the lay anyway.

"There are commercial possibilities here."

As you know hens will always run home when danger threatens. If you are out driving and you see some hens pecking about by the road and their hen house is on the other side you can be sure that if you approach quickly they'll take the suicide route and run right across you. And that was the theoretical base for this diversification.

The henhouses were right across the road from the workshop. And, being on the inside of the bend in the road, the farmer could see the cars approaching from each direction while he was at his bench. When a particularly promising looking car approached he would wait until it was just opposite the Dutch barn (if it came from the left) or the big tree (if it came from the right) and then release four hens from one of the cages he had for the job. He would then give a loud blast of the Klaxon he had salvaged from an old steam lorry. The terrified hens would bolt home across the road. Hopefully one would be run over, whereupon the negotiations would start.

As time wore on those hens grew to be powerful layers, the product of an exhaustive programme of line-breeding and developed pedigrees, which all helped the cash-flow.

I was reminded of that story when we had a surprise visitor at the discussion group this Sunday. It was Big Fergie the oilman who, when he was in Aberdeenshire, bought a struggling small farm and a struggling sawmill and made them both work in the modern fashion. Fergie shocked those few of us who knew the difference between South Africa and the rest of the Dark Continent by emigrating there in 1989.

Of course we shouldn't have been shocked. It was even then becoming obvious that serious attempts were being made

there to treat all Jock Tamson's bairns as equals whatever colour their mothers were. Anyway, Big Fergie never gave us any reason to think he was especially sensitive or especially liberal. He's the sort of man who will call a spade a 'spade' if he wants to and who may not mean a tool for digging.

Anyway Big Fergie is back looking for a house in Scotland.

He just couldn't take the culture shock of South Africa. Like the Do It Yourself gardening programme. This showed how to lay a crazy paving area round your barbecue. It showed how to get three black men to prepare the ground while one was breaking the paving stones, another was laying a nice even bed for them and a sixth was mixing the cement. The man who was Doing It Himself didn't move a muscle except in his mouth.

It's the sort of DIY I could stand. It means Do It Without Contractors but you don't need to get your hands dirty yourself.

Big Fergie didn't think that was right. And he had a run in with some of the neighbours over his own gardening efforts. He'd been working with two African gardeners when the blazing sun suggested a beer. The good manners with which

he had been brought up ensured that there were three beers but that didn't suit the neighbours. "That's not the way you treat them," he was told and a lot more. That led to an interesting debate on the equality of man before God and ended with Big Fergie saying "Well that may be what you do but I've bought this land and as far as I'm concerned, mate, your standing on a little piece of Scotland here and in Scotland, if one drinks, we all drink."

Of course there is tension all over the place in South Africa and that includes quite a bit between the English speaking white settlers like Big Fergie and the white tribe who have been there for over three hundred years... the Afrikaners. The white settlers have a nice line in abuse of the white tribe to the effect that the white tribe are slow intellectually. It's really the same as our Irish jokes.

And it was one of those that reminded me of the roadside chicken farmer.

This driver ran over one of Van de Merve's chickens and flattened it. Scared half to death because of the farmer's reputation as a man of passion, the motorist took the flattened bird up to the farm and asked if this was one of his chickens. "No, no." said Van De Merve, "My chickens are more sort of round."

Recreating the hey day of the small family farm

THERE IS a brave new attraction in Aden Country Park near Peterhead. It is a working farm of the type for which the thinner lands of Buchan are famous and where her hardier sons were brought up to be grieves on the big 'fairm toon' and to go forth and people the British Empire.

Hareshillock was quite typical. A small two up and two down house with windows stuck out of the roof to give a bit of clearance in the bedrooms, an L-shaped byre and barn, and a couple of railway carriages for storage and maybe to keep a few hens. But what is remarkable about this modest sixty acre place is that they moved it stone by stone from it's original site to the country park and then rebuilt it, exactly as it had been on its original site.

The only differences are, that instead of being in the typical bleak Buchan landscape, the farm is now set amid the mature trees of what was once the Aden Estate, that the fences all look a bit new, that there is no great heap of rusting metal round the back and that the docks and nettles haven't really got going yet.

Now, the interesting thing about Hareshowe is that it is to be a working farm. The idea is to recreate an era which was the hey-day of the small family farm and which they date as between 1935 and 1955. It covers the period of transition from horse to tractors and of course covers the war and postwar years when those small farms, while they may not have been goldmines, were very comfortably off.

And now they are looking for a man to work Hareshowe, using the technology of the period. There'll be no combines, for example and no cattle courts. The harvest will be taken with the binder, the sheaves, the stacks and the steam mill. The fattening cattle and the house cow will be tied in stalls all winter and fed untold barrowfuls of turnips. There'll be no eating their way to springtime through a pit of silage.

But the hurtful thing about the whole deal is that Fiona (who is usually a loving and supportive companion) suggested that I would be just the man to be employed in this working museum. "After all," she was unkind enough to say, "You're still using all the old fashioned methods."

It was a bit unfair. After all we have a most modern harvest with combined harvesters, grain drier or sealed grain tower, big bales of straw and two co-ops through which to market the grain. But Fiona was nearer the mark with the cattle this week for I have taken some of my cows back into the byre.

As part of my campaign to sell my Jersey cows, I have taken some of them in and tied them up in what used to be the Dry Coo Byre. At least it was supposed to be the byre for dry coos because it hadn't been passed by the sanitary as fit for the production of saleable milk. The inspectors used to think it was funny how the air line went round the corner from the milking byre and into the Dry Coo Byre but they could never catch us adding the milk from the 'dry coos' to the cans which rattled off to Aberdeen every morning.

I've thoroughly enjoyed having my little byreful of cows. They are now trained to stand round the right way in their stalls and have grown to love me because they know that I have come to give them food and to brush them down. They love me even more when I bring them water for the waterbowls aren't working. Anyway when you're not trying to squeeze the last drop out of tied cattle it makes for a much more savoury environment to keep them just a little bit short of water. Anyway the silage soup I am feeding them on has about as much water as they need.

So twice a day, there I am back in the days of the graip and barrow. I use the old grieve's formula. As much as you can get on the barrow, between two beasts twice a day. They get that first. Then I muck them using the same graip and into the same barrow. It was always the way but I don't know if the sanitary in their madness would like that in a dairy nowadays. Then I offer them not too much water carrying the pails from a trough which is not nearby, and then I sweep up before giving them a groom. How fine they look.

I have been reminded of what we have lost in no longer being able to take the Tilly lamp round a byre of tied cows in winter. The sight of the forty patient ladies all sat down chewing... crunching their way though the cud... giving their regular volcanic rifts of methane. Their heat and the smell of milk and muck and digesting silage were a welcome to the byre. The weather might do its worst in those days but there was always warmth in the byre.

Of course they were a lot of work. It is fine to have four Jerseys tied up for a week but forty for a winter was some sentence. That was forty barrowfuls of silage and forkfuls of straw to be made into more barrowfuls of muck. And if you were hand watering forty beasts you knew the weight of a pailful of water.

Of course there were ways of mitigating the toil. Like the loon who explained that if you put a little bit of muck in the water you could make a bucketful do several beasts instead of just one. And the old terror James Low who as grieve terrorised this farm for over forty years enjoyed telling me of the time he gave the baillie a weekend off. On the Monday he came across the poor man red in the face and at the mucking. "What a muck there is this mornin," he said.

"That's funny," said the grieve, "I hadna any all weekend."

Harvest signs are not good

SCLEROTINIA AND alternaria stalk the land of my forefathers. Don't ask me what they are. All I know is that they are the reasons my oilseed rape crops this year have a dark brown tinge to them, that it is difficult to do much about it at this stage, and that there is nothing good about it.

And I can ill-afford even minor disasters.

My man from Financial Control Services says I made a profit of fifteen thousand in the year to June 1991. My accountant says it was only six thousand but of course he is doing a different job. The accountant is trying to make the farm look hopeless to reduce my tax bill whereas the other chap is producing management accounts which have to be sufficiently hopeful that I don't give up in disgust. That would put him out of a job.

Anyway, what's nine thousand pounds when it's only figures in a book and only relevant to a year that is past... and past remede?

The really interesting figures are for this year coming; those are the keys to my survival as a farmer.

As the all-important harvest approaches the signs are not good. They are trying to talk about £101 a tonne for barley off the combine and last year we got £106, so there goes one of my thousands. Then the oil seeds are being quoted at £220 against £265 last year at this time. That should make the accountant smile for it would mean nothing at all for the taxman.

But will the taxman give me anything back if I make a loss, for such seems very likely? I have said nothing yet about yields. And while the barley and wheat could be up to last year the brown rape cannot equal last year's thirty-one cwts per acre.

Now you would think that a man who was in the same discussion group as all the premier Grain Barons in Buchan should have no difficulty with crop disease. Surely Mossie will keep me right?

Well, yes and no. Yes he'll tell me what to do. But no, not till it's too late. He was free with the advice that my brown rape was produced by my failure to spray with Ronulin as well as Compass. Of course I had no idea what I had or had not sprayed with as I leave that to my crops consultant and the contractor, but I do keep records and sure enough.

So what should I do? "It's far too late now. By the time you've counted off the damage the sprayer will do at this time of year you'd be as well jist leave it." I know fine that the reason for that advice is that every time Mossie drives into the village he likes to look at my parkie on the braeface and admire the deepening brown as it turns to black. Of course he assured me that he there was no alternaria at Mossside and I believed him.

Until Sunday. The great man didn't turn up at the discussion group which gave us a chance to discuss how tiresome we found his success. It was when I wondered where he would be that Crookie, another of the Grain Barons, said "Oh, I ken whar he is. Him and the Red Rooster are seein about a helicopter to spray their rape."

I can't compete.

So where is my crust to come from? Hardly the cattle surely? Well, there may be some hope. I have almost

115

cleared last spring's calves out of the house at weights up to 326 kilos deadweight and that compares with last year's effort in putting them outside and bringing them in again and finishing them for Christmas. That must be an improvement. And the grazers have started to go fat though they seem slower than last year's. There has been plenty of grass this year but it seems to me that sunshine is more important to the fattening cattle. The old men used to say "a warm back was more use than a full belly" and as usual there was some truth in what the old men said.

They were better bought this year or at least they were cheaper. Big for the money, all continentals, they averaged 106 pence on the spring day.

That's six pence less than last year and yet my buyer says they are the same quality. Mind you, he only has a scale of three... that's good cattle, decent stirks and plain brutes. Mine are decent stirks as last year's were but with so few classes you'd think there could still be a quality difference.

The cows could certainly do better next year. I surely won't have a death rate above ten per cent again if I farm on for a hundred years. The latest

such disaster concerns the cow I told you about the other week. I bought her at the mart. A snip at £580, she was an enormous cross Simmental with a five cwt Belgian Blue bull calf at foot. She was rough mind, badly in need of worming and tired after her voyage from Orkney. After Orkney she would surely thrive on Ardo's gentle braes.

You'll remember that I got a phone call the night she came home to say she was staggering around. It was milk fever and the vet saved her with ease and I thought no more about her except what a bargain she had been.

Until last week. She was lying there quite dead one morning in a pool of her cud. The vet thinks she went down with milk fever again and falling head down hill drowned in her vomit. Nae fine.

When I chinned the man from whom I had bought the cow he paid me off with a first rate story.

A well known dealer from Maud had sold a crofter two fine calves both of which died. The crofter came angrily at the dealer who spoke thus; "Man ye've had bad luck. But it could hae been worse. I sold your neighbour two calves just like yours... and he died."

Not the time for finer feelings

THE HASH is on. The last of the pigs have gone to market with honour; the cattle are going off fat too, or with mastitis; and, with the sun beating down out of a cloudless sky and a parching breeze rustling the standing crop, the salvage of 1991 has at last begun.

We started on the fourth of August, about ten days later than usual. And we started this year, not with the winter barley but by swathing some of the rape. That was not because it was riper but because it was so diseased. As you know I have been leaving the worrying about that sort of thing to my crops consultant so I am far from being an expert in plant pathology... but I'm learning fast.

My rape has sclerotinia, alternaria and damage from light leaf spot. This disease meant the pods were beginning to shatter and spill the seed of Ardo to the four winds... so we had to cut it down. The field that slopes down to the village and is therefore seen by everyone was particularly bad and turning black in patches as my embarrassment deepened. I found Mossie having a look at that field one day and I asked him to tell me what was wrong with it.

The great cereal grower shook his head sadly. "Disease, Charlie. Disease."

"Oh aye, what's it got?" said I eager to learn.

"What a mess. You've aathing here except aids."

I thought that a somewhat tasteless remark but it was not a situation which lent itself to finer feelings. We've now swathed most of the rape and while there is quite an impressive bout of straw the grain is a sorry twisted sight. I'm hoping to be only 25 per cent down on last year.

There is only one bright spot among the oilseeds and that is in what I call my perennial rape. That's the crop that I didn't sow... I just looked after the volunteers that came up after last year's harvest.

117

That crop is full of weeds but it is practically disease free and while the others are swathed it is still green and growing. It's Cobra and so is showing a nice big pod which cheers me up as I drive past.

Now I am sad for Aberdeenshire but it is true that I am not alone in having diseased rape this year. In fact only my natural modesty stops me from admitting that there are a lot worse crops than those at Little Ardo. But how has Mossie got on in this difficult year? Has he earned the reputation he owns of being an agronomical crackshot? Or is it just that he's not easy to beat for 'blawin'?

In hopes to find that his success had been found out this year I sneaked over to Mossside for a look when I knew he

would be away at the Turriff Show. There were several others there who knew about Turriff show and what we saw took our breath away.

From the road it looks like some sort of French beans grown on huge bushes. It is obvious that he is trying something out because at each tramline there is a change in the crop. These are plots and each one better than the last.

It's not just that the plants are six feet tall but the pods are huge... they are crammed with seeds. In fact I am sure the one at the far end is a six rowed variety. And it's all so clean. Where my poor twisted Tapidor pods are shattering, Mossie's pods are rubbery and green. Whereas mine was dying before the sun came out this year his has been burgeoning in our Indian summer.

The stems are green. I didn't even realise that rape stems could be green. I thought that by harvest time they were all a mosaic of blacks and browns but it is an exceptional plant at Mossside that has one speck of black.

In short the two tonne crop must be on. And if it is on at Mossside it must be possible at Little Ardo. Though I have to take over the Chemical Spraying Company, I'm going to go for it... next year.

This year it is salvage time. And it's not just the rape. We have the worst wild oats this farm has ever seen in the spring rape, by far the worst day nettles in the winter wheat and the first barley we cut was like a nature trail. In fact the mayweed, cleavers, docks, sterile brome as well as grass had taken so much of the nitrogen from that crop that Mossie suggested the few seeds we did salvage might go for malting. We've got over two tonnes to the acre but less than two and a half so we'll need some such luck to get our money back on that crop.

For all it is an unrewarding year for me I am enjoying the salvage. It is a good time of year. There is a buzz in the countryside. There is never a shortage of something or somebody to speak about. And I enjoy the people who come about the place but once a year. Like Sandy who drives the swather owned by Mossie and the Red Rooster. Sandy's a first rate operator and is reckoned to put at least a hundredweight on the crop. Some drivers ruin four bouts round the outside while turning. The standard ruination factor is three but Sandy seems to be able to damage only two bouts. That means he's well worth the beer one has to take out to keep him lubricated. And the poor man needs it for the swather has a tiny sweatbox with no air conditioning.

On Monday I couldn't attend to Sandy's thirst as I was driving home the grain (And the sticky Willies and the mayweeds) but I needn't have worried. The field he was in is about half a mile long which meant he was at its foot every three quarters of an hour. And at the bottom of the field is a public house. When I eventually got down to see him I found a well worn little trail over the dyke. He was probably in for a glass of water... or two.

Farm dreams which fell on stony ground

ONCE I had a dream. I would farm the ancestral acres with style and aplomb. I would hire consultants to tell me the best way to grow crops and when to spray them with what, and when autumn came I would bring home harvests that would make the previous tenants of this hill look down in envy.

The work would be done with all the best machinery too because I would hire contractors. I would be saved the expense of the £90,000 combine that swallowed my crops. I would be saved the bother of reading all that junk that comes in about new chemical sprays. My life would be one of ease, punctuated by some unde-manding but fulfilling work like stacking bales, gathering stones, taking cheques to the bank, and feeding cattle sent home by my cattle consultant.

For the first two years after my return from Africa the dream seemed to come true. I grew three tonnes of wheat and barley and a tonne and a half of oilseed rape. There were even profits.

The harvest of 1991 has been a sad awakening.

I told you last week about the winter barley that I hoped might go for malting because it was so choked with weeds that it must be short of nitrogen. Well it didn't malt. It had some-how managed to get 2.25 per cent nitrogen despite the com-petition. That diseased field of rape yielded almost exactly half of last year's average.

And I have another record to report;

Not only do we have the best wild oats we've ever had, and the prettiest Mayweeds but in amongst the finest stand of day nettles there has ever been on this hill we have a wheat crop which is almost com-pletely wiped out by take-all. I didn't notice that as soon as I might have because you couldn't see the wheat turning white as it was down below the canopy of green nettles. I once had 19 cwts of wheat with a bushel weight of 40 pounds so there is a formidable record there for the beating but I think this year's crop might be in with a chance.

It is in years like this, when the loss is so much per acre, that I am grateful for the smallness of this farm.

This farm glowers across the Ythan valley at the farm of Wardford. In the days when there were men on farms, Little Ardo's lads used to argue for hours about whether Wardie's 40 acre park was as big as our biggest one which was almost 21 acres.

And the keen rivalry didn't just infect the men. The farmers too would pull out all the stops to beat the other. That was espe-cially true at harvest time. There was great competition to be started first, even if it meant cutting the corn with just a shade too much green. And when Wardie's lads started to lead the sheaves home the cry would go up "I see the craws are nestin' at Wardford." If we fin-ished first, which was always on the cards as we had the south facing side of the valley, my father would do his best to run into James Presley so that he

121

could remark casually that it was far too late in the year to be harvesting. If Wardie's got the binder in first Mr. Presley would be making extra trips to the village in hopes to catch John R. Allan to ask if the rats had been at his binder cloths.

Now, among the many sea changes that had hit our industry is one which has put all those old wisecracks right out of date. And it's not just that we don't build carts like crows nests any more, or that we don't keep rats nowadays to eat the binder cloths we don't have either. But the whole idea of being first is quite out of date.

The man who is first is the man with the poor little crop or the one that is full of disease... the one that dies first. The trick is to keep your crop green and growing and filling for as long as possible.

That truth was brought home to me the other day when I heard someone boasting to Mossie that he had started to combine his winter barley. Mossie was quite unimpressed and unsympathetic. "Oh aye," he said, "We used to grow crops like that."

That is the key to the hope that while this year's harvest is going to be a disaster it may yet be less than a catastrophe. The first field of barley yielded a bit over two tonnes, but things improved until we were beginning to kid ourselves on that we were approaching the three tonnes. The rape started off at 16 cwts but that was certainly the worst crop. The rest will surely reach the tonne. And while the take-all has meant an early and a light harvest for the one field of wheat, the wheat across the road is looking good. It is still green, growing and, hopefully, filling.

Nevertheless my dream of leaving it all to consultants has been shattered. If it is to be a question of harbouring disease and growing weeds I can surely manage that myself and save the expense. And it's not that the advice was necessarily wrong. The chain of communication was too long. The consultant told me what to do. I told the chemical company what to send. When it arrived I told the contractor to come. Then, if weather did not permit, it could be a few more days before the job was done. And because I was only the message boy I was not giving my fields the constant and careful attention I would otherwise.

So I've not renewed the consultants contract... and I've bought a sprayer.

Piggies now our only hope

BACK IN the hands of the bankers. That's what I fear most as a consequence of this year's poor crops. I have been managing with bank finance from seed time to harvest and even in straightened circumstances a skilful farmer can handle that sort of debt. But I don't see how we can survive in the current climate if we need the banker to finance the fixed capital on the farm. I have tried it and I can assure you it was no fun.

I took over Little Ardo after a few years of my father's retirement-in-residence. He had been a good husbandman... the land was in good heart... but there were no livestock, the machinery was lamentable, and there hadn't been a new shed put up since they built a new barn in 1945.

In a short time I built three

sheds. I built the cattle numbers up to 700, and I built up the overdraft to a quarter of a million. I enjoyed the cattle. I was very proud of the sheds. But the £1000 an acre of debt fairly took the fun out of farming.

What really put the tin lid on the contract was that when I was at the height of my folly my father announced that he would like to get to hell out of it and move to the sunny south. I would just buy him out. Then the interest rate went up to 18 per cent except that, as a poor risk, I was actually paying over 22 per cent.

I knew I was in trouble when I started to get invitations to lunch with the high head-yins of the bank in Aberdeen. I quite liked that mind, because it was nice to be in company where mine was a small overdraft, and these bankers do live well. I deserved the free lunches too. There was one year in which, with the aid of one man, I earned a trading profit of £20,000 but the Bank of Scotland needed £37,000 in interest payments to finance expensive lunches... and I also had an overdraft with the Clydesdale as well as cattle from the Mart at three and a half per cent above base rate.

I shudder at the memory.

As I predicted last week, the first crop of rape was the worst. Most of the rest yielded a tonne to the acre and the perennial rape, the stuff we didn't even sow, yielded 25 cwts and so brought the overall average up to the tonne.

What a bonus the perennial has been. We saved £15 worth of seeds. We saved on all the autumn cultivation and drilling which was another £30 or so and we put on an ocean of muck instead of the usual three bags of compound fertilisers. Then in the spring time we put on just 90 units of nitrogen... half the usual dose in case this volunteer crop would be full of disease and go flat. And yet it not only out-yielded the rest... it yielded a profit. It does rather baffle all the science we put into the job these days.

Of course the reason for the comparative success of the volunteers is that they were Cobra and all the rest was Tapidor... and this has been a disastrous year for that variety.

Anyway, a tonne per acre is half a tonne down on last year. That's £143 an acre down. And then the tonne will make around £30 less so we are about £173 an acre down. Over my 80 acres of oil-seed rape that is £14,000 which is enough to wipe out the whole of last year's profit with still the disaster of the take-all in the wheat to assess.

So how am I to stay out of the clutches of the bankers?

The cattle hardly look promising at the moment and the pigs could hardly be a weaker market. But oddly they are the only hope.

With the help of Gowkie, my neighbour who knows his cement, and Potions the New Deer chemist who enjoys a bit of farming free of the overdrafts that normally go with it, I have put up my capacity to fatten pigs from 200 to 350. And with the market flat on its back I've managed to get the first 200 weaners home at 83.9 pence a kilo with some hope that the remaining 150 due home this week may cost even less.

Now it is but a few short months since those animals were selling for 123.9 pence a kilo. If only the price will rise to that level again during this year I will be able to recoup my harvest losses. It may not be a realistic hope but it is the only one. And who said farming was realistic anyway?

The piggies are doing their best. They are off to a flying start. They are deep bedded in the new season's straw and re-ally a picture. Now is the time to show those who fear for the welfare of farm animals round.

Mind you, Mossie is unimpressed. I had mixed the cement for the platform which holds the pigs drinkers and, with an eye to the cost, I used an ungenerous mixture of sand and cement.

It took Mossie half a minute to spot the patch of loose sand underneath the water bowl. "T'hell's this!" he exclaimed with his usual delight at the mistakes of those less gifted than he. "Is this desert pigs ye're gettin, like? Oh, the pigs'll love this. Snoots into this sand and burrow the lot oot. You'll have a desert storm here I'll guarantee. Is Stormin' Norman comin ower tae open the new piggery, like?"

Of course he is absolutely right. Snouts in like desert moles they are demolishing the platform at the rate of several feet per day. And they seem to be sharing the work. Even on my last tour at night when nearly all is quiet. There are a couple of lads on night shift snorting and heaving out the sand.

There's not much I can do now till they finish.

My fear of the banker's clutches reminded me of the

farmer who was coming home from Turra show. He saw the banker out walking a yappy dog. The farmer stopped the gig and did what we have all fancied doing from time to time... he gave the banker a thrashing.

"What did you do that for?" the banker asked, a little surprised.

"Well it's a gie cowardie lad that goes home frae Turra Show withoot a fecht."

Turriff neep hits page one

IN 1939 when the rest of the world was holding its breath to see if Hitler would give in to the great British ultimatum to get to hell out of wherever he had got into next... to see if it would be peace or the outbreak of another World War to end wars, the North East had weightier matters on its mind. The Aberdeen *Evening Express* is said to have led its front page story with the heading "Giant turnip found at Turriff".

I was, of course, less than a regular reader of the paper in those days so I cannot say for sure that that story is true. But it does have the essence of truth about it. It is part of our strength as a community that we keep our own perspectives on things.

I was reminded of the famous headline this week when the great events in the Soviet Union were unfolding. I was most affected by the whole business; dread induced by the

news that Gorbachev had been overthrown; fear that the whole apparatus of repression and persecution was to arise again; the incredible bravery of Yeltsin as he attempted what seemed like the impossible.

It was like the great speech Garibaldi made when he offered the mere thousand remaining of his beaten army only blood, sweat and tears if they would continue to fight for the unification of Italy. We could only read about Garibaldi but we saw Yeltsin on that tank. It brought tears of admiration to my eyes.

And the tears were back. Tears of hope for humanity at last when the Red Army pulled back from the gallant but pathetic barricades.

But then I've been weakened by a university education and long periods away from the North East. Big Hamish is a truer son of this soil. It was his reaction which recalled the giant turnip.

In great excitement at the end of the coup, I phoned Big Hamish to tell him the news. "The gang of six are running away to the airport to try to get a plane out of Moscow. Yeltsin has sent the Russian police to arrest them and Gorby's on his way back to Moscow. It's all over Hamish. What do you think of that?"

There was a longish pause. "Well now, I dinna ken if that's a good thing or no. I bought a hale tank o' diesel on Monday thinkin the price would rise. If there's nae tae be ony war or ony threat o' war the price'll likely gang doon." There you have it. That is our strength. Let the world go hang we'll keep our eyes on the things we know and the things we can do something about.

And Hamish does know about machinery. He's bought himself a wonderful new spraying rig (for "an undisclosed five figure sum") and has got off to a grand start with that. You will remember that, by giving up the pies he used to eat between meals, he has taken off over six stone with no loss of mobility. He looks altogether a younger man and when he went out spraying with the new rig the farmer who lived a bit away but knew Hamish well asked him where his big brother was.

At any rate the new sprayer means Hamish has a sprayer to sell and he's trying hard. After the disaster of my weed and disease control this year I have decided to do my own spraying and Hamish believes his old Hardi is just the job.

I've had my first lesson which goes along with the trial of Hamish's machine.

Refusing to learn the lessons of history I have sown another 33 acres of rape and they must have their pre-emergence spray.

I have terrible fears for the whole exercise. Mossie tells me I must put on one pint to the acre. But the can is three litres. Worse than that, the machine is calibrated in litres, and Hamish knows only how many litres of water we need to the hectare. That would be all right but Hamish (the man who claims to have no idea how much a per cent is let alone how many you get to the pound) insists on doing the conversions for me and does them very quickly indeed.

Mossie tells me the rape will not grow if there is any overlapping and how do you ensure that when there are no tramlines visible yet? Well the answer is that Potions and Big Hamish stand at each end of the field and stick in electric fencer posts at the correct intervals. All I have to do is run them down.

That seemed reasonable until we came to the gushet. This ran the length of the field and narrowed from about 30 feet to 10. How on earth would we manage that as the switches for controlling how much of the booms were firing were all broken?

Before I had time to think that one out, Hamish had bent the ends of the booms round at right angles and was roaring at me to get a move on. I was half way down the straik when I realised that this system meant that instead of some overlapped rape getting a double dose I was giving some of it five times what was required.

Mossie just shook his head. "Some o't will grow... maybe" he said.

All the same I think Hamish and I will have a deal. The only thing between us is the value of the old Hardi. Hamish is at £2,000 and I am at £800. He has indicated that he will move and I haven't yet told him that I too am flexible. In the meantime the sprayer is in my yard, so what's the hurry?

Entire car fleet was at the Inn

THERE'S A certain head of righteous indignation getting up in the North East about malting barley. Of course it is of no direct concern to me as my Puffin had 2.25 per cent nitrogen and I don't grow any spring barley so it is a matter with which I can claim to deal dispassionately.

You see Danish barley is being imported at a rate which is not known but is thought to be alarming. The Morayshire crop is light and full of screenings and the maltsters are turning to Europe for their main ingredient. This leaves the spring growers more than somewhat aggrieved. They have seen the lugubrious adverts for Scotch whisky made from the finest Scottish barley and have grown spring barley despite the tiny yields available in order to supply the scotch market. They are unamused at being told that the stuff they have grown is only fit to feed livestock.

And how can the maltsters get away with it? If the main ingredient of scotch is to come from Denmark can we really say it is scotch?

If the French grapes are not so good one year, do they import grapes from Cyprus to make the Beaujolais Nouveau? No, of course they don't. French wine has its good years and its bad years. Everybody knows that and adjusts their prices and intake accordingly. It all adds to the spice of drinking French wine. They even have a body which writes 'Appellation Controllee' on their bottles to make sure that it is genuine. Buyers don't need to fear that their Chateau Mouton Rothschild has been made with grapes from the Ukraine just because they are cheaper and farmers in France are not asked to feed their grapes to pigs when they have a bad year.

If our trades descriptions acts aren't enough to stop them calling Danish whisky 'scotch' then maybe we need a body to 'Controllee' our whiskies and

give the buyers the assurance of its Scottishness... I should think it would help them sell the stuff.

Anyway, enough of politics. I really wanted to tell you today about two of our worthy farmers in this area. They specialise in the malts. They both grow large acreages of spring barley to supply the great distilleries of Speyside and beyond. But while they are heavily involved in the production side of the malting trade they are perhaps best known locally for the enthusiasm with which they embrace the consumption side of the business.

It is a sad thing that many of the finest brains in our industry have failed to reach their full potential because they were sidetracked by drink. Indeed my friend James Fowlie has often said without prejudice or malice of any sort, "When the drink starts to interfere with the business... give up the business". The trick is to remain unaffected enough by the drink to recognise the point at which the trade-off between consumption and production has become critical.

There are those who suspect that the farmers of Upper Whitelees and The Brock may be reaching that sort of crisis. I don't agree but have to admit there is some evidence in what happened at what should have been the start of harvest this year.

Upperton and Brockles had had a particularly jolly Friday night at Duncan's Inn at Inverurie. They'd been selling sheep at Thainstone and Brockles was celebrating a trade that was far better than it might have been while Upperton was drowning the sorrows of a trade that was far below his needs.

At closing time the two heroes decided to leave their cars and take a taxi home. That showed how sensible they were and as they were neighbours it would be no bother for Upperton to come round with his wife's car and pick up Brockles to take him down for his car in the morning. As it worked out young Brockles was there too so the three could have brought home all three cars.

Once down to the tavern, there being no great hurry to get home and the drink of the previous night having helped them to prodigious thirst it was decided that the three would just have a swift one to clear their throats and put a cheerier face on the day. That worked fine until at closing time, they were again faced with the problem of what to do about the three cars. It was decided to take a taxi home and Brockles would take the wife's car round in the morning and pick Upperton up and take him back for his car.

But when on Sunday morning they were back at Duncan's Inn there seemed no better plan than to go in and have their morning as the harvest was hardly ready yet. And at closing time they took a taxi home. The plan was that Brockles would appear in the morning and take Upperton down to the pub on the tractor to make a start to get their four cars home.

That would have been only fair as Brockles' wife would need her car for her job in the town. But again it didn't quite work out. To cut a long story short, and to illustrate the point about drink interfering with business, when the harvest day came, neither Upper Whitelees nor The Brock was ready to make a start. All their plant was down in the car park of Duncan's Inn.

132

Mossie's Convoy Capers

THE ONLY event of note this week was the rough time the lorry drivers gave Mossie when he was delivering the first of his wheat to the Aberdeen Grain store at Whiterashes.

Now, as you will know, lorry drivers as a breed don't care much for the collection of dirty, unsafe and unlicensed tractors with which they have to compete at harvest time. And it's a problem that's getting worse for, with harvest now lasting from late June into October, even the biggest farmers have waiting periods when there is nothing better to do than to yoke the Grey Lady and play at road hauliers.

Not that that's the case with Mossie. He's properly tooled up for the job. In fact he's got a cart that looks like a ship's boiler on wheels (and probably is). It holds no fewer than seventeen and a half tonnes and takes up a good deal more than half the road between Mossside and the grain store.

Wednesday it was and Mossie was making sedate

133

progress along the narrow roads and causing something of a hold-up. There are passing places on those roads now but Mossie, in common with most farmers around here, believes those are to let him overtake slower cars when he is zipping along. He doesn't see passing places as being anything to do with the serious business of driving your grain to market.

Not that he could see, for the mirrors don't come anywhere near far enough out to see past the great load, but by the time our hero arrived at the grain store he was at the head of a very impressive convoy. I say impressive but that is not to say that the drivers of the ten lorries forced into stately procession were impressed. They were flashing their lights and waving their fists and altogether acting in a dissatisfied manner.

Now, anybody else would have been sensitive to this mood. They'd have realised that these professional drivers could feel aggrieved at him not only taking his business away from them but making it a slow job to get on with the rest. Not Mossie. Instead of hiding his ticket showing that he had delivered seventeen and a half tonnes he showed it off to the lad behind him who had just come in with his ten-tonner.

"Oh, nae use. Ten tonnes? No, no. Of course I've got the expensive licence. Mine costs £30 a year. How much is yours?"

Now Mossie is not an ignorant man, though he does seem to do things occasionally which lack wisdom, and he knows perfectly well that the licences the lorry drivers have to pay cost them £30 every second day, so he should not have been surprised that he was jostled by the angry mob before he got back to the tractor and away.

Aye, the world's ill-parted, thank goodness.

For my own part the oilseed rape is brairded and looking well despite the seven week drought and the fact that I only sowed three kilos to the hectare instead of the recommendation of twice that. My theory is that there isn't room for all those plants and I don't want them to waste energy killing one and other when they should be concentrating on growing. And we've swathed the spring rape which, I am very relieved to say is looking really average, unlike the disastrous winter stuff.

That meant a visit from Sandy who drives the swather and another busy evening for me carrying beer down to him.

Mind you, by half past nine I had forgotten him and was being bored solid by the tele when the door bell rang. It was the Red Rooster who (with Mossie) has a half share in the swather.

The Rooster was on a high. Where was the swather? Was he finished? What like a crop was it? Had Sandy gone home?

Forgetting that other people have lights on their farm vehicles I opined that he must be away home by now but agreed to take the Rooster down to the field to see for himself. That meant a trip in the Rooster's springless little Japanese van along the endriggs of two ploughed fields and through a park of stubble.

Now I've told you before that the Rooster is one of those farmers who was once young and who hasn't yet realised that the top figure on the speedometer is a maximum not a target. So, as we skimmed the tops of the drills and bumped over the last years tramlines I asked the Rooster if he still did any competitive driving. I think he may have misinterpreted that as a request for more speed and to my great alarm he accelerated, a feat which I would not have thought possible. "Well I am thinking of starting again", he said.

"Well for God's sake don't start till we're round this corner." He hadn't seen the corner of the field looming nor did he realise, as I did, that it was a sharp gushet-neuk. Brakes, handbrake, change-down and foot to the boards, and we got round somehow without getting down below fifty miles an hour. The only casualty was my supper, but what a way to live.

We found Sandy, a blaze of light, still working away. And as we waited for him to cut the winter swath I asked the Rooster where his partner was. "Mossie? Oh, he's the thinkin drinkin partner. I'm the workin partner."

I believe him too, though that's not quite how Mossie puts it. When the hash was on in August the Rooster was so excited that when Sandy had had enough of the swather at half-past nine one night the Rooster took over and drove all night until Sandy was ready again at seven. That afternoon the Rooster went to his partner and told Mossie that it was his turn to drive all night.

"Oh, no ye dinna," said the bold farmer of Mossside. "I'm the sleepin partner."

September 23, 1991

Now the blawin can start

OH BOY! At last I've got something out of this harvest to blaw about. We have 11 fields of crops and we had to wait until the tenth to get a decent one... and it could even be a record.

You may have noticed that there has been a dour and even desperate note in my diary this last few weeks. That has been down to the harvest which has been below average to say the least. And we farmers need the harvest to give us a source of blaws. It's not that we won't blaw about anything we do but the harvest gives you so much to blaw about. There is the yield, there is the wondrous dryness, the speed with which the crop was won and the bushel weight. The weight is particularly good fun as the bushel has now been discarded in favour of the hecto-litre and only Mossie even pretends to know what that might be. Yes, you can blaw about each of these things and multiply your blaws by the number of fields you have in crop.

Harvest has always been the main annual source of blaws. The old grieve who terrorised Little Ardo for more than 40 of the middle years of this century used to tell me without a blush about the great crop of oats he harvested in 1921. The stooks were so thick that when it came to the leading there was no room to get the cart into the field so they had to back the horse into the gate to get the first load. Then there's the Red Rooster who had such a bold crop of oilseed rape that he had to take out the top riddle from the combine because the seeds weren't getting through.

Of course I'm not saying that all the blawing that goes on at harvest time is strictly merited by the crops we reap. I like to tell of the wise old man who was asked what was the biggest crop of oats he'd ever heard of. He answered "Fourteen quarters. That was at the Station Hotel at Mintlaw at aboot half past ten ae Friday nicht." No,

No. We don't need great crops for major blawing but we do need something to work on. And in this respect this harvest has been a sore disappointment.

In fact so bad has the harvest been in terms of yield and quality that we have been turning our taste for humorous fantasy to a sort of competitive gallows humour. At the discussion group that meets at the Salmon Inn on Sunday nights there has been a competition to get attention by telling worse and worse stories of this year's disasters.

I did quite well with my story about trying to get a sample of our first field of wheat. It is the one with the fine stand of day nettles and the take-all and the sharp eye-spot. I needed a sample to see if any seeds there might be were dry enough for the combine. The methodology is to pick a few heads, rub them hard between your hands to separate the seeds and then blow away the chaff. The trouble I ran up against was that when it came to the blowing away the chaff the corn was so light that it blew away as well. Eventually I had to pick out the chaff from the shrivelled little crines that passed for a crop.

Then there is the story, also true, about the artic that was hired by one of our biggest and most successful agri-politicians to take off oil-seeds direct from the combine. It was there all day and left without a load. I don't think I believe Mossie's story about the farmer who cut rape all day with his combine and then took all the seeds home in his tank. But it is true that the farmer who now has the once famous farm of Collynie (where

137

John Duthie-Webster made a fortune out of shorthorn cattle) just walked away from some of his rape crop.

Yields have been down and so are prices and there is no doubt that in this part of the world we are down £100 an acre despite the savings in overtime and fuel in this easiest of harvests

All that changed on Sunday though. We had our last field of Riband wheat to cut and it looked well from the road. No weeds, no lodging, no greens. It would surely run three tonnes even in a poor year. It's a 17 acre park and the combine holds four and a half tonnes in its tank. As I ran happily back and fore to the steading I did my sums. It looked like 13 loads which would give me the three and allow for a bit of blawing that night.

But then I gradually became aware that something was not as it usually is and indeed that that was good. I twice found the combine waiting for me when I got back with an empty cart.

Then the tractor seemed to be labouring in bringing the cart out of the field. When I realised we really had a crop on our hands was when the combine driver stopped giving me a load on the move on the grounds that the discharging auger wasn't winning. Anyway we ended up with 17 loads and a bit (the bit grew bigger as the evening wore on).

At the Salmon Inn that night I was in full flow about my four and a half tonnes to the acre, plus what the combine cut while discharging and plus the 'bit', when Mossie insisted on putting his metre (which by bad luck he had in the car) on the sample (which by bad management I had brought down to show the lads). "23 per cent. You've cut a tonne o' water tae the acre."

Even so I must be close to the four tonnes. By next week I should have the exact details from Aberdeen Grain and I'll be able to tell you what went wrong. But in the meantime there's no holding me.

Farm walk was a day to remember

I WANT to tell you today about a heroic farm walk we had here 17 years ago. It was the one and only time when I have drunk whisky out of a calfie's pail.

But first a bit about the week that's away. It has been a boring week. Nothing has gone seriously wrong and nothing has made a serious dent in the financial gloom surrounding the farm. I still haven't got the final weights for my wheat though I can say that my four tonne crop is down to nearer three and a half tonnes with half of it away to the merchants. The spring rape is not yet all away but it was cut at 15.6 per cent and has yielded over a tonne. None of the pigs or cattle has died.

There has been nothing to do the spirit good or fill the blood with fire for a great future. Not like that fine summer's evening in 1974 when we enjoyed a farm walk here with the gentlemen of the New Deer and District Agricultural Discussion Group.

Little Ardo was much in demand for farm walks at that time because I had been a pioneer among the new breeds of cattle which had come flooding in from Europe. We had Charolais, Simmentals, Gelbvieh, Chianina, Romagnola, Marchigiana and Blonde d'Aquitaine. For good measure we also had a few South Devons as somebody had told me that they were the only British cattle which could compete with the continentals. We even thought about a sign proclaiming at the end of the road, "Charlie's Safari Park".

The New Deer lads were the first farm walkers for many years and so there had been a great redding-up for the visit. I think it was then that we discovered that underneath the mud of ages there was a fine cement close at Little Ardo. There was the most infernal bonfire of years worth of manure and feed bags and binder twine and rape and ruck nets which had been thrown into a corner of the piggery following our last traditional harvest 15 years before.

The walk had to be carefully planned to show the old place off to least disadvantage. We had to be sure to pass the field of winter wheat that was looking particularly well but to steer well clear of the winter barley in which the contractor had tried out his new seed drill. The machine had been very impressive but seemed to need a rest every now and then. That meant that there were strips about 100 yards long with some very backward reseeding which looked awful. Of course I didn't know the Red Rooster then or I'd have known what to do there. When faced with a similar disgrace he surrounded the bare bits with white sticks and called them rather grandly "My Plots". There was the problem of showing off our new Dutch barn without letting them see the 18 pneumonia victims (refugees from our barley beef factory) which were pining there.

Then there was the machinery. Our guests were all progressive farmers who had the best of tractors and my sons who went to school with their sons pleaded with me to hide our tractor fleet. That consisted of two old Fordson Majors... one of which had a safety cab and one of which had a rear loader which could fill a small barrow at one go. I felt bad about it but I hid them anyway.

When the tour was over I had arranged for a couple of crates of beer, sandwiches, and a couple of bottles of whisky to aid our discussions. As it was a fine night, we decided to have this discussion on a ring of bales on the grass in front of what was then my parents' house. They were away on holiday, so they missed the fun – which was just as well.

The beer and the sandwiches seemed to go first, and my guests were quite complimentary about what they had seen. Though one did say that the only way he could see the Gelbvieh being dual-purpose was if you rode it after the hounds and then fed it to them.

And, of course, there was some stout defence of the native breeds against this continental invasion. My guests guessed that the meat from these great big brutes would be coarse, and that they would take an awful lot of feeding.

Anyway, as the evening wore on the conversation became catholic – as did the taste for drink. Gradually, sale was

found for the whisky. And then the beer seemed to be a slow way to get your word into the argument, and everybody was preferring a dram.

Now that caused me some small embarrassment. At that time we didn't have many glasses, and anyway it was not my house, and it was locked. The beer had been all right out of the bottle, but the whisky demanded a vessel.

I had a stockman at that time called Gordon, and he was particularly resourceful in questions of liquid refreshment. When two of the discussion group went down to the village for more supplies, Gor-don disappeared then re-appeared with half-a-dozen cal-fie's pails, more or less washed, and said: "This'll dae for me onyway." Five others took Hobson's choice with a good grace and the discussions got going again.

By nine o'clock we had exhausted our interest in cattle. By ten o'clock we had got fed up of agriculture. By eleven o'clock we had sorted out the national and international political scene, and by midnight the good people of Methlick were being entertained to the most enthusiastic renderings of the old ballads, carried down to them on the evening dew from the farm on the little hill.

I am glad to say that they all went home and that they all arrived safely. But they were not all intact. One highly respected and extensive farmer arrived home wearing a rather snappy Italian slip-on shoe on one foot and a potato crisp packet on the other.

We found the missing shoe half way up the beech tree my father and I planted in 1946.

Pigs are crazy over concrete

TODAY the good news is that the Spring rape ran almost as much as I thought and that if the field had just been a wee bit smaller we'd have had a tonne to the acre. With growing and harvesting costs of £80 that leaves something for the overheads.

The bad news will take a little longer.

I have told you about the 200 pigs that I fattened for the Grampian Country food group. They took all the risk and gave me £4.25 a pig for each one that reached the slaughterhouse alive. We had two batches and the whole 400 survived and only one needed so much as an injection.

I could see that the only thing that was standing between me and a fortune was the money to take the piggies onto my own balance sheet. Not only that but I would extend the shed and keep more.

The 350 arrived in good order and immediately began to suffer. Those were not the old environmentally friendly piggies that we'd had before but factory-produced weaners who didn't really understand the principles involved in straw-bedded courts. They were used to concrete and were certainly not going to do anything so intimate as their toilet among all that rustling stuff and insisted on using the raised feeding and drinking areas. With great difficulty and a lot of sweeping I've finally got that cured after five weeks or so but several of them still prefer to sleep on concrete rather than snuggling down among the fresh straw.

Whether it is the pleasant surroundings or not I don't know but my 100 per cent survival rate is burst. I have a new statistic to monitor. Along with my feed conversion rate, and my growth rate I now have a rate of attrition. That stands at one per week.

Now Mossie, my guru in matters porcine, made me shudder once with his telling of the piggie that managed to tunnel free from his shed and disappear into the oil-seed rape. It was a tale which many of the other listeners found hilarious. I could not find the prospect of wading up to my chin in yellow flowers listening for grunts and shouts of 'over here' and 'over there' every time there was a rustle in the rape. Eventually they just had to leave him till harvest time.

Well now, it was when I had discovered my biggest dead pig that my worst fears were realised. It had been quite a struggle. He was in the farthest away pen and I had to wrestle him through his 197 pals. Through a gate, past his 150 neighbours and out at the gate which leads to freedom. The last hurdle is two 12 foot gates tied together with some unwanted electric cable. It was with a great sense of relief that I closed that gate behind me and went off for a cup of coffee.

I was at my books when I heard Gladys, our treasure, shouting "Charlie! There's pigs in the close." And so there were. There were also pigs in the cattle crush. There were pigs in the byre. There were pigs off on the road to Methlick. Indeed there were pigs everywhere except in the pen... they had all taken the chance to escape from that damned straw and get back to a decent concrete base.

I had forgotten to tie the gate. What a row I'd have given anybody else who had done such a thing.

My second thought was, "What luck that the rape is cut", but on that score there would have been no worries. My piggies didn't like to leave the concrete so it was surprisingly easy to get the them nearly back to where I wanted them.

It is a sad truth of pig keeping that a pig can squeeze through a hole much smaller than itself in order to escape. But it is an even sadder fact that no matter how many times you enlarge that hole the pig will not go back unless it wants to. Nevertheless the gallant Gladys and I did get them back. We just worked away at it edging them closer and shutting off escape routes. We eventually got them corralled with half a dozen gates round the door of their shed and, when they became hungry, they went back. It had been a sweaty hour.

And even worse news is what has happened to the discussion group. We have a fiver kitty to defray expenses and the idea is that when it has built up

to £100 we'll have a ladies' night with a barbecued pig and the wives there. We were nearly there until things went badly wrong on Sunday. I only heard about it as I had left early, but in retrospect I should have seen it coming. As I left Mossie was saying, "I'll just hae an orange juice this time… and put a gin in it", and then when the barmaid's hand was at the optic, "Gie it twa pushes, Anita".

Apparently Big Hamish got out of hand after that. He's celebrating because whereas the rest of us have a third less rape this year he is up from eight cwts to 16. "There's nane o' ye can beat me. My yield's doubled". Well now, Hamish went on the Zambuccas. That's a high octane drink into which you place three coffee beans and then set fire to it. After it is heated up a bit you blow her out and knock her back. But no one told Hamish about the blowing-out bit so that after letting the fourth one heat up too much, the fire caught his breath. The resulting cough set fire to his sideburns and the fiery water swept across the bar and down onto the carpet.

There was no real damage except to Hamish's lips and to the date of the ladies night. I estimate the night of the Zambuccas has set that back at least a month.

Shame of Cruelty Man's call

DISGRACE HAS been heaped on disaster.

We have had a visit from the cruelty. It is the first time to my knowledge that they have ever been at Little Ardo. I suppose it's my own fault for keeping donkeys but I am not proud of the visit.

At first I felt I had let down the great men who went before me in this farm but I soon shook that one off. My great-grandfather John Yull could hardly point the finger at me after driving his gig home from the mart hanging on to the mare's tail. And that saintly man, my grandfather Maitland Mackie bade his grieve, the great James Low, to saw the horns from 33 year-old Ayrshire stots he'd imported from Canada. Old Jimmy found the stots unwilling to be still enough for the saw which was perhaps not unreasonable of them given the unavailability of anaesthetic. So he used the broom cutters and whacked them off. After the first horn they normally went down with shock so the second was easier. When he was finished the midden was running red and Jimmy lived in fear of Peterhead prison for a week. Until the worst of the week was over he put the men to dig up the road to slow the inspectors down.

Of course it was only done because they were tearing one another apart with those nasty sharp Ayrshire horns and none of the stots was even ill after the operation but it would hardly be attempted today. And you can't blame old Jimmy. In the 30s, if your boss said 'jump' all you could do was to ask, 'How high?'

But old Jimmy wasn't blameless. He used to dishorn our calves, as everyone else did, with a red hot poker. No calf ever grew horns having had Jimmy's attentions at three weeks old. And he insisted they didn't suffer. He could tell. Or so he said, because they were so relaxed after the initial jump as he burned through the skin. So confident was he of the painlessness of the deal that he didn't even use the anaesthetic when it was freely available.

And yet it was my treatment of Gina and Dominic, the cuddies, that brought the cruelty inspectors to Little Ardo for the first time.

I had been hiding in the house and struggling with my Vat return when a young lass of maybe 18 came to the door. She had read about Gina in the *Glasgow Herald* and would like to look at her and her foal. I was delighted, but I really didn't want to leave my bench and told her where she would find the donkeys.

Off she went and returned after a while saying that she had seen Gina and would like to buy her. I told her that one donkey about the place was at least enough and that I would not have been hard to deal with but for the fact that Gina in fact belonged to a cousin of my father. It was agreed that I would ask whether I could sell.

When the lass phoned back I had to tell her that I was sorry but Gina was not for sale.

"When are you going to sort her feet?" came the aggressive response.

"Well now, it seems to me that that is between me and Gina," said I, "but since you ask I will tell you that I am intending to do it on Saturday for I know they are needing it."

The phone went dead and I thought no more about it till two days later. When I returned from the mart on Friday there was a note from Gladys. The

cruelty man had been to see the donkeys. He would be back sometime and his name was Russell.

I was displeased. And I was especially displeased that Mr. Russell should think that the only reason I would do my donkey's feet was because of the threat of the cruelty. I phoned him up and explained that I was going to do Gina's feet the next day so if he was going to come and see them he should come immediately. I wanted him to see just how bad they were.

The cruelty man who came was in fact a lady and a very nice one. She said the donkey was 'beautiful' and 'fine' and we agreed that she was needing her feet done. It was a not unpleasant visit and it didn't faze me at all but I do think there is something wrong with the system which allows a young twerp who knows very little about anything, anonymously to summon up the powers that be to investigate people who have offended them.

It didn't matter in my case but it mattered a great deal to a neighbour... also in the horse world. She was accused, anonymously, of feeding a dead foal to her pigs. That brought the cruelty, the police and the sanitary inspectors down on her riding stables. She now has letters from the authorities saying that there is not a word of truth in the accusations but she regards that as small consolation. The seven horses she had had boarded with her left and she puts that down to the phantom caller. After all, horsey girls wouldn't like to stable their horses at a place where they might end up in the swill.

The dangers of anonymity are highlighted when you consider that it might have been a rival stable trying to destroy her reputation... and succeeding.

Annual harvest of stones

I AM into the overdraft window. This year's harvest is in the bank and, despite the poor yields, the overdraft is temporarily paid off. So rather than watch the creditors gather we went off to Rome for a few days.

Honest to a fault, I have to admit that Rome was a bit of a disappointment. We didn't go all that way to see the Pope but we made sure that on Sunday at noon we were among the misguided souls gathered to receive his blessing. I use the word misguided, not in any spirit of religious bigotry, but geographically. As we gazed up expectantly at the window at which those who had been there before told us he would appear, a most unsaintly voice told us in many languages that we would now hear a relay of the ceremony the Pope was holding

149

for the faithful somewhere else. The hungry sheep looked up and were not fed.

I was glad that I was not a devout Catholic who had sunk his life's savings in expectations of a blessing in St Peter's Square.

Apart from religion, people go to Rome for art, archeology and architecture. We decided we had no time for the art so we would stick to the other two and they also made me sad. We started at the Colosseum, surely the finest sports ground the world has ever seen. Of course its main sporting contests seem to have been battles to the death between the prisoners of war and between wild animals and people who worshipped what were regarded as false gods... like Jesus.

I found it made me slightly sick to stand in the arena and think of all those spoiled brats that were the Roman citizens enjoying the deaths of the tens of thousands who were sacrificed to their pleasures.

Now, we all know that Imperial Rome fell on difficult times in the Middle Ages and suffered multiple pillaging. But what made me sadder again for the place was that when the renaissance of classical architecture came they got a great deal of their stones and their facings in particular by plundering what was left of Imperial Rome. That means that when you go to see where Julius Caesar planned to overcome our Pictish ancestors you are into archeology rather than architecture. Though there are many pillars still standing or being set up again much of it is just piles of historic stones.

It was worth a look but soon it was back to my own historic stones at Little Ardo. We seem to have an inexhaustible supply of those and each year when we have made ground for the cereals there have always been tons and now there are tonnes of them to be carted off.

Old Jimmy Low, the last grieve to rule Little Ardo's roost, used to tell me that he hated taking off stones because it didn't matter how many cart loads you lifted, there would be just as many the next year. Of course, that may indeed be so and with the bigger modern ploughs going ever deeper it does seem like there is no end to the stone gathering. But I believe that you can win. Our home fields which have been carefully managed for the longest and which have always had the lion's share of the muck have now a tolerable admixture of stones. You might get a bogie load in every ten acres. No one will convince me that when the first sods were turned in the 18th century they didn't have a lot more stones than that to deal with.

We have two bits of field which are in more like the primeval condition. One is very steep and the top end of it has maybe a bogie load to the half acre while the flat area at the bottom has few. And the other is like a quarry. There would be four bogie loads to the acre after the plough, four more after the ground is made and another couple of loads after the seeds are sown. But I keep at it in the faith that my children, or perhaps my children's children will be able to sow seeds there and only turn up nine loads of stones to the acre.

In fact it is because of the long term positive nature of stone gathering that I rather like the job. It is hard work of course and jumping in and out of the tractor is very hard on arthritic knees but it is unique in farm work. Most of agriculture is cyclical. You do the same thing each year and when the year is over you set about doing it again. If you spread muck on the land the grass thrives on it and you make silage. The cows then make it into muck and you have to put it out on the fields again. It is repetitive and it is hard. It is the wonder of peasants like us, and it is our strength, that we stick at it.

But with stone gathering it is slightly different. It happens every year on the thin lands of Buchan but as I lift each stone and as I coup each cart load, I can say to myself (and I do), "that is a job done. Those stones have been tidied up and they will never obstruct the coulters again".

And there is another reason why I am enjoying the stone gathering this year. I am doing two jobs at once. In a below average piece of planning we have erected the pigs feed bin round the back of the piggery in a cul de sac. Any good driver can get round there but even the best have trouble reversing out. So far there has been one wrecked strainer, one torn-off bumper and much bad language. So instead of throwing the gatherings into the wood this year they are going into making a turning place for the feed lorries. It should save me many's the red face.

Alchemy of the Boy David

THE FULL extent of the disaster that was my harvest is now quantified. In financial terms, I am down 28 per cent or £16,000. That would be serious even to a big farmer if farming were profitable but to me and in the current state of the industry it is alarming. After all, my costs are up and my total profit last year was only £15,000.

However according to my accountant (The Boy David) who is young enough still to have some faith, all is not yet lost. Because my year ends in May we know already what our main income for the year will be so we are left with eight months in which to do something about the looming loss.

Costs have to be cut.

First we have sacked the crops consultant at a saving of £700. Then we sacked the contractor who did the spraying.

That saves £1,500 though it needs a bit of perverted accountancy. The new sprayer has cost me £1,500 so what's the profit in that? Ah well now, according to the Boy David, that counts as capital and so is not down the drain the way paying a contractor would be. Fair enough but surely my labour costs me something.

Then there are the piggies. They only produced £1,000 as their contribution to overheads last year but the current batch look good for £3,000 and with average luck (but then I never seem to get that lucky) the next batch are supposed to give me another £1,000.

Then I'm getting some help from the discussion group. Crookie the Grain Baron has a bargain boatload of urea from somewhere behind the Iron Curtain. They want his seed potatoes and as they have no foreign currency they are paying him in urea. That and the swing to spring oil seed rape, will save me £2,000 off my fertiliser bills.

I am going to save a bit on depreciation. I'm not buying any other machines than the sprayer so my machinery will be in the books at less. It won't mean our old scrap goes done any less fast but as there is less in the books there will be £600 less to be written off the profit.

And another strategy has occurred to me as I write. If I sell the drier, of which I am fed up as our local co-op dries our stuff so cheaply, and the post-hole borer which is costing us over £100 a hole up till now, and both power units I bought for the drier, I can put money in the bank and further reduce the depreciation. In fact if I sold everything I would not have anything to depreciate. Far better in theory but perhaps not in a very good theory.

Then again, because I put my grain into our grain co-op to be dried this year rather than drying it myself there is a saving on my fuel bills of £1,200.

That is all the Boy David's alchemy that I understand, but what it means is that if I can deliver on his budgets, there will still be a profit of £10,000 this year. Isn't farming easy?

Even Mossie has been having a rethink in the light of the poor growing season this year and the changes envisaged by MacSharry. Having made a considerable reputation for himself in the old days when the EEC encouraged us to produce as much as possible by giving us prices way above what our combinable crops were worth, he is now chasing the subsidy and cutting his inputs.

At least that's what he says he's doing, but I can't see how he can think his first move cuts costs. He's bought himself 90 stots so that he can claim his £2,900 Beef Special Premium. I have quite failed to persuade the great man that what he can lose off 90 big stots can dwarf the £32 pounds a head. Then there's the linseed. Oh yes! No European subsidy is to be left untouched in our man's new philosophy... he's going for this £240 pounds an acre to grow the crop that could sell for £100 in a good year. Of course he knows a bit about growing linseed having baled some and thrown it in a quarry a few years back.

Big Hamish is the only member of the discussion group who is not looking at economies for the coming year. He's had a fabulous year at his hobby... contracting out his dear machinery. He has baled over 10,000 big bales of straw for a start. But even he has been helpful to me. He has shown me how to overcome one of the handicaps of having old instruments in a one man band.

One of the banes of my life has been tractors that wouldn't start without a tow. Of course auto-start works for a while but there comes a day when the only way to start the old Major is to get someone to give you a pull. I wouldn't have thought it possible to start a tractor like that in a one man band but Hamish showed me how it is done. You pick up the thrawn machine with the fork-lift. Make a head of steam and then let her down onto the cement with a bump. When the old girl starts to fire you lift her wheels off the ground again so that she doesn't take off into the great unknown. I haven't tried it yet but I'm going to.

In other ways the discussion group have been covering themselves with something less than glory. Crookie has a car which finds it hard to pass a pub and a pub with a petrol pump irresistible. The other day he pulled into the Thumb of Gartly for petrol. He was there for four hours filling and still ran out of juice on the way home.

And Mossie's behaviour has been so far below even his average that the wife, the very soul of understanding and patience, wasn't speaking to him. This went on for several days until he phoned her from the pub. When she answered he saluted her with a not unfriendly "Aye noo. That's broken the ice."

Ancestor solves my problem

I'VE BEEN sorting through the early months of this diary for a book which will be out shortly. It is great to have such a vivid method of looking back. It is quite salutary to remember an event and then look up the diary of that time to see how it felt then. It is amazing how the memory differs from the record. It makes me wish that I had (as my 25 year old daughter has done) kept a diary all my life.

Anyway, with nothing to do on the farm but wait for winter, and now that I have got that away to the printers, there is time to take stock.

My first column told that as I returned to the family farm I was stepping in behind a long line of improvers. There was William Yull whose drainage work earned him a medal from the Royal Highland and Agricultural Society. Then there was his son John who installed the first water closet in Aberdeenshire so that the tenant of Little Ardo could flush before the Laird, Lord Aberdeen. That caused his successor to say "There's aa' thing here but siller". He was the first Maitland Mackie and he built the piggery and the byre.

Little Ardo was then one of the barest places in this bare part of the North East called Buchan. My father, who called Buchan the 'Cold Shoulder of Scotland' because of the way it sticks out into the North Sea, gave the old place a mantle of trees so that in the wildest of nights there is now some cover and in summer it is heaven.

I said in that first Diary that there was much to be done if I too was to be remembered as an improver, so, after two years, how am I doing?

I am afraid it doesn't come to a lot. I've got within one load of readymix to linking the steading and the four houses on the place with cement and it seems that even with the shortage of cash caused by last year's poor growing season we'll manage to complete that this year. That'll be getting on for half a mile of good road where once there were bumps and potholes.

Then I have put in a bulk bin and feedline at the piggery so that we can feed 300 pigs automatically while loose-housing them on straw. We've made quite a nice job of that with raised feeding and drinking areas and a loading bank whose race has three handy doors to hold the piggies in convenient lots for loading.

Also we knocked down one wall of John Yull's barn to make it muckable and so usable as a cattle court. I felt bad about that though as the keystone of that gable had 1857 chiselled into it and we broke it in the removal. We must get it back up somewhere... soon.

The trouble is, where would you put it? The whole of the old steading is falling down. James Low, the great grieve who ran the show for three generations of my family, came here in 1933. He told me that William Yull's old steading built round the midden was rotten then. It is still rotten, and the roof will no longer patch because the sarking would not hold a slate let alone the man who climbed up to fix it. Maitland Mackie's piggery is rotten also though we can still fix away at that.

And the old byre is only 12 feet wide. What can you do with that in a modern set-up? We've got it as a cattle court but I've had to buy an old illegal cabless Major with a rear loader that takes about a barrow load at a time to let me muck it... and with its leaking roof it needs mucking too often.

There is no doubt that the old steading needs demolishing if we are to be a successful and easily run business here. But we are more than that. We are part of a family tradition and part of a farming tradition and part of the tradition of Buchan. If we sweep away the couthy old steading we are sweeping away the toil of our forefathers. And yet if we don't we are making the job of survival on this hill more difficult by the day.

So what am I to do?

Uncannily, I have had some help in making up my mind from beyond the grave and from an ancestor who was steeped in our traditions.

I have told you before that among my father's papers I found a number of novels in various stages of completion. Well the first of those is about to be published and it deals with exactly my problem of how to reconcile a regard for heritage and the needs of modernisa-

156

tion.

There is a young man like me who is besotted with tradition and an old man who has lived it. The young man proposes to re-open the old well from which early generations of the family had drawn water for the stock and for the house. It is easy for me to see why the young man would want to do such a thing. It is a beautiful stone-built affair with troughs running off it and flagstones worn by the feet of his forefathers.

But the old man has nothing but contempt for the idea.

But "it was made by your grandfather's father." said the bright young man in whom I see myself.

"It was that. But he's died noo. Nae doubt he thought he was clever but I did better."

The message of the book is that the true tradition is our working of the land, not the monuments we erect upon it. I need no further justification for modernising Little Ardo. All I need is about £50,000.

Grain Barons simply clam up when the note-pad and pen appear

I SAID last week that there was nothing to do but wait for winter. Well I must modify that. There is plenty to do because winter seems to be upon us. There is frost in the air and steam on the breath in the clear mornings and there has been an undue proportion of those wet and windy days which caused a friend of mine to say, "It's on days like this that I'm glad I'm a lawyer in Aberdeen and not a sheep up Strathdon". I really need to get the calves spent before the cows start to get too thin. It is a funny thing but it seems that if you let your cows get thin at this time it is very difficult to get the swagger back on them until Dr Green reappears in the spring.

And then there is my programme of winter sprays.

You will recall that, after growing some of the poorest rape crops ever and some of the finest stands of weeds in Aberdeenshire, I have sacked my crops consultant and bought my own sprayer. *If you want a job done right do it yourself*, is to be my new rule.

That is a rule that has worked well for many but, now that I am hard up against the day of action, it fills me with fear.

Which sprays should I use? My plan was to earwig on the grand conversations between the Grain Barons in the discussion group that meets in the Salmon Inn on Sundays. From the safety of my crops consultant's recommendations I was always hearing the Red Rooster or Crookie shooting off on what we needed being any spray but the one I had paid for. Even Mossie, who plays his cards so close to his chest we're not sure even he knows what is in his chemical cocktails, let slip the odd hint from time to time, so I thought I would easy manage without the consultant.

But the trouble is that they all speak so quickly and I forget what it is they have said. I know they would clam up completely if I produced a note pad and wrote everything down. So I have adopted a cunning approach. Every time I reckon I have got a tip I rush off to the toilet to write it down. I haven't cracked it yet though, and the mildew is just starting on the winter barley.

I shouldn't be surprised that it is difficult to pick up the ideal spraying programme from the rich and famous. After all, they know what they are talking about and so when they are discussing what to put in a tank they don't spell it out like an instruction manual. Most of the mixture is well understood by the experts and they only discuss the wee adjustments which make the difference between excellent and perfect. My needs are more basic.

Mind you I'm not the first person to be confused by the Grain Barons. There was a time, perhaps a dozen years ago, when it seemed that the North East was to become a great grain growing area. With the advent of the winter cereals and the Common Agricultural Policy, and with our long hours of summer sunshine it seemed to many that the breadbasket of England might have something to learn from Aberdeenshire where four and even five tonnes was being grown between the stones.

I expect the Barons were trying to be helpful to their English brothers but I'm afraid they found us a pretty difficult lot. From their sophisticated, computerised and metricated world it was a great leap backwards to come to Aberdeenshire to learn.

One such student landed in the asylum, it is said. He started at the Red Rooster's where they were told the formula for getting a fine clean crop was so many *pints to the acre*. Well, to our friend a pint was something you drank in a pub and an acre was a measure that had been used in the olden days about the time of the Magna Carta. He then went on to Crookie's where another beautiful crop had been produced with so many *pints* of this and that and the *leftovers-from-last-year* of something else.

But our visitor finally flipped when he came to Mossside. Mossie was at that time preparing a field for measurement for the *Guinness Book of Records* and the man from the south was naive enough to ask for chapter and verse. He got it. But the basic measurement was *tins to the fill* (of the sprayer) and the real secret was a *coffee cupful to the fill* of something said very quickly.

I suppose all this means that what we have here is as much an art as a science.

I am afraid that the choice of chemical is not my only problem though. It has never occurred to me to bother too much about those tramlines the contractor always left in our fields. As he did the spraying and put on the manure it hardly seemed anything to do with me.

Maybe it's because he now has no interest in tramlines, I don't know, but my first year of doing my own spraying is going to be be-devilled by the most bizarre tramlining I've seen.

The winter barley isn't too bad. As long as I avoid the false starts and put some stakes round the missed bit I should have no great problem. There is only one set of tramlines missing apart from the outside and of course it is not a problem to see where to go there. But my two fields of oil-seed rape have no tramlines at all, and neither have two fields of wheat. Maybe that is only fair for in the two fields that run beside the road down to the farm there are tramlines everywhere as well as gaps between passes. At one part I counted eight out of 23 rows missed.

I know we need to move to low input farming but that is ridiculous. Those fields look like some sort of pattern for a new tartan and I feel a high level negotiation coming on.

Amazing speed of new dog

I HAVE done it at last. I have bought a dog.

Trying to keep beef breeding cattle without a dog has beaten me at last. It was all right for my father for he had six men and they all had children to help with the herding. But now I am a one man band it is just too much without a dog.

That means I have to leave things till the weekend when I can get help from Potions the chemist. That isn't really good enough when you need the vet and it's no good at all if you want to use artificial insemination. You can't be sure that your cows will run at the weekends.

I told you about the awful day last year when we were taking some stots home from the grass I take from an old widow a big mile away. After being through several of my neighbours' fields my complete humiliation was only avoided by the intervention of the Fyvie Bus which appeared, lights flashing and horn tooting driving my stots back.

Well, I was at it again this week. Seven young bulls had to come back from that field. Even with a squad of four and after weeks of training them to follow a North Eastern Farmers bag we arrived home with only four. Two landed back in the field from which they had been removed and one broke a leg jumping in among some heifers and had to be destroyed.

I had realised that I really needed a dog since the day some 15 years ago when I had had a terrible merry-go-round with a red Hereford stot. He ended up at Uppermill of Tarves... some five miles from home... among the country's top herd of Shorties.

Fair disgusted with my cross country stint, I set off to collect some calves from the now cereals convener with the National Farmers' Union of Scotland, David Jack, at Rothienorman. It took me some time to find Henry, the cattleman. Now if Henry was an excellent chap then his dog was even better. And when I eventually found our man he was bringing 40 heifers home from a field a couple of miles away along a B road which includes at least one nasty T-junction, and the entire staff was Henry and his dog. There was no excitement, no anxiety and no despair. It was all quite unlike my herding and Henry wasn't even on foot. He was bumping along on an old grey Fergie.

Still I resisted getting a dog. Since I was bitten by that Scottie when I was four I have always distrusted dogs and they, no doubt sensing my discomfort, have never liked me.

With the arthritis in the knees making cross-country cattle chase more and more impractical, I did last summer speak to my old pal Captain Ben Coutts about a dog. He agreed that with my fences and my knees and the kind of cattle I keep there was no use me going for a dog at below about four hundred pounds. And he agreed in principle to helping me find one.

But I don't know if I ever would have got one had it not been for Potions. He saw his chance and went and bought it. I told him what a capital thing that was and that the two of us would just get the cows in and spend their calves with the help of the dog.

It's one of the three wheeled variety called Honda. Potions calls it a three wheeled bike but that is a contradiction in terms. Anyway it is now my dog and with it I can take cattle from anywhere on the farm to

anywhere else though I cannot go on the road.

The Honda will go absolutely anywhere else though. And the speed is terrifying. I've only been in two gears so far and there are three quicker ones. The cows and calves were scattered along the Howes and among five fields in all and yet we had them rounded up without any effort in as short a time as it took them to trot home. It careers up the one in two-and-a-half braes and splashes through the swamp caused by the burst drain that is my only concession to the wildlife. We haven't discovered yet at what angle the dog tips over but no doubt that will come. The only time of any difficulty was at the gate to the steading where they had to pass their minerals and their straw and their magnesium syrup. There some of the old dears thought they had done enough.

At first it looked as though there might be a break out. But as soon as I remembered how a real dog works, and had got that explained to Potions, he then tore back and fore making darts in at their feet and we had them. In what seemed like no time we had the calves wormed and warm and the cows which needed it wormed and outside again.

What a success. And at no capital cost for the dog belongs to Potions. I have a friend in Kansas City Missouri who has a lawyer friend whose hobby is having and driving a combined harvester. The lawyer cuts my friend's crop for the sheer pleasure of it. His advantage is better than mine with the dog but then I am in a smaller way of business.

Unfortunately the cows are more loving mothers than I had given them credit for. Twice that night I was up putting them back on the braes. They even demolished one of the intervening gates.

That made me think that maybe Potion's Honda wasn't so good after all. A real dog could have been tethered by the gate to snarl at them and keep them back. And then I thought... "well it's worth a try and who's to know?

After I had replaced the gate I left the Honda guarding it with the engine running. In the morning my dog was asleep but the cows were still in the park.

Honda the dog is a real boon

THE DOG called Honda is proving to be a real boon. Instead of half an hour trailing my poor old arthritic bones down the Brae and along the Howes every morning to check the cows, I roar round on the amazing three wheeler. And there is just nowhere it cannot go and there is nowhere any cow I want to take in can hide from my tireless, speedy dog. Before I had her my heart used to sink when I saw a beast in a far field that needed attention but now it is less than a problem; it is my chance to play Chris Surtees in pursuit of Geoff Duke.

I have only fallen off once so far and that was in the most bizarre circumstances.

I told you that my contractor, having neglected to give us tramlines in the oil-seed rape, had given us so many tramlines in the wheat that as much as a third of the field was unsown in places. Well now, as the crop has become stronger and therefore easier to see, it has become apparent that that is not the only disaster. When the drill machine was almost at the end of each pass, the driver had started to turn leaving a neat triangle (about three square metres) unsown. It wasn't the waste that worried me, it hardly mattered in a field so full of tramlines, but the triangles were all down the roadside and clearly visible.

Furious to the loss of all reason, I enlisted the help of Potions the chemist who came down to play on Sunday, and we set about re-sowing the triangles. It was late of course but maybe by summer time the second sowing would catch up enough to hide my shame.

We yoked Honda the Dog to the task. Potions would drive while I sat behind him facing backwards with a bucket of wheat between my knees throwing handsful on the muddy earth.

As we sputtered and bumped it was a pale shadow of my forefathers' elegance as they swung rhythmically along on foot sowing out of the happer in the olden day. Nevertheless there was still something of the elemental in this method of mechanised handsowing. *"We till the fields and scatter the good seed o' er the land"* I sang, though I knew that God's almighty contribu-

tion was most likely to be frost which would delay germination until the pheasants had got all the good seed.

Potions, though, was buoyed up by the optimism of youth and was all for going for the garden rake next. He would drive Honda up and down while I would hold the rake out behind. Ten passes or so and the good seed would be covered.

That would have been done had it not been for the Dog's extraordinary acceleration and Potion's poor driving. We were just about finished the sowing when, for reasons that will forever be his secret, Potions opened the throttle and with a roar Honda's back legs leapt forward and overtook the front ones. The seedsman landed very smartly on the ground and waited in terror for Honda and Potions to land on top of him.

But fortunately the designers of the Dog had taken care of that. The inexperienced drivers among us are always giving her too much gun and having her rear up alarmingly but she can't go right over. When she gets up to or about the perpendicular the back hits the ground and stops her.

I was so thankful for that that I insisted that the exercise be abandoned and the seeds be left naked and to their fate. I'm taking Mossie's advice and getting the college advisers to come and assess the loss caused by the bad sowing, so any improvement we had been able to make would only reduce my compensation anyway.

Mossie and the other Grain Barons are off to Smithfield next week. The Red Rooster wants to look at a new stripper attachment for his combine with an eye to the Linseed market, Crookie wants to sell some seed potatoes. And Mossie? Well he just wants to be there.

The discussion group got round to the Royal Smithfield Agricultural show this Sunday and, fortunately, some of the doings to which the lads got up in London do bear telling. Like the time in the night club when the romantic duet was about to be sung. To heighten tension, to add to the romance, they released some of that smoke that spreads around the feet of the artists and lends an air of the ethereal or even the heavenly.

But the atmosphere was totally destroyed by Mossie. When he saw this smoke curling up from under the stage he whipped off his jacket and shouting "Fire, fire!" started to beat at the source of the smoke. Having accepted the man-

agement's invitation to leave, the heroes would take a taxi. No bother – one was hailed, but there were five of them and the driver refused point blank to take five. Eventually Mossie saved the day, "Its aa' right lads you take this taxi and I'll meet you there."

That was fine. The four set off in their taxi and Mossie would get another and meet up at the place to which they were going next. They had gone a mile or so when Crookie saw the flaw in this apparently reasonable strategem. "How can Mossie meet us there when we haven't decided where we're going yet?"

It was indeed a problem, but the lads' mood was so jolly and their concentration span so short that they decided to forget about the farmer of Mossside and proceed to the Farmer's Club. They were right not to worry for when they were swishing down Lower Regent Street they heard a tap-tapping at the rear window. It was Mossie. He had slipped quietly into the boot of the taxi and travelled, if not in style, at least with a certain panache. London cabs have boots that open down the way and he was able to leave it slightly open and pop up to wave to the lads.

166

Cash is all there in the courts

IT'S ALL in the mind of course, but I have the unfamiliar feeling that, despite all the evidence to the contrary, we may yet survive.

I have at last had some luck with the cattle. This year as a whole has been quite horrendous with cow after cow turning up its toes with a mysterious disease which now seems to have been nothing more than milk fever. With the nasty wet weather there wasn't enough in the grass and they probably died of calcium deficiency when the milk started to flow in early lactation.

Now five cows may not be a lot when you set it against the great sweep of history but when you have only 33 in total, a total which must be maintained in order to qualify for hill cow subsidies, it's a lot of cows. And that isn't the only cause of attrition among the breeding stock. I culled another five because their udders or their fertility was away. Those were all Jerseys and all a fair age so while they were not a big loss in one sense, they were in another, for they were not greatly sought after in the farrow ring. That is a big snag with the Jersey hill cow... a farrow cow price of less than £200.

So what on earth makes me think I can survive?

Well, there are a number of things apart from my natural optimism.

There are the pigs. We have just 80 out of the 350 to go and the sums are looking good. They cost 82.9 pence a kilo as weaners, that's £25 a piece. The first lot made 97 pence and the biggest lot made £1 a kilo. I don't yet know what the feed has cost me but Mossie says I will have made £10 a head at them. That is almost a quarter of what I lost at harvest time so things are looking up.

Of course it is nothing to how Mossie has got on with his own pigs. When the market heard that the great man's piggies were ready it jumped from £1 to £1.15 a kilo and once again he doesn't know what to do with his money. It wouldn't be so bad if he kept his successes to himself.

Anyway, I'm pleased with my £10 a head. It vindicates my decision to adapt the old piggery for loose-housed fattening. It also gives me a great start in the new venture of taking the risk myself instead of fattening them for the Grampian Country people. They were paying £4 a piece so I could take a holiday now and still be ahead.

The only smart thing I did in cattle this year was to buy thirty Black Hereford heifer calves in Spring with a view to bulling them next June.

They cost £65 in April and did well on the milk. I put them out in July onto some silage aftermath and they are outside yet, apparently thriving on what grass there is left and two pounds of beef nuts a day. They must be about four cwt and look to be on schedule for the bull in June. And certainly they don't look dear.

Then there are the feeding cattle. I'm afraid I haven't done them very well... again. I take this quite appalling old Yorkshire foggage from a widow-body who lives a mile away. It could be ideal for my cows but they have to stay on my 'less favoured area' land to get the subbies. So I put my grazers there and they didn't do well.

They are all inside now and chewing through the barley but

I fear some of them are going to miss the Christmas market whereas, if they had all been done right, they'd have been away off the grass. But it's not all loss. Though they have been slow to fatten on the foggage the poor rations have given them time to grow. Cash may be long in coming but it is all there in the courts and I can go out and count it any time I like. When you are still enjoying the overdraft window at the back of harvest it is easy to be patient and enjoy the sight of a few stots turning the grain mountain into the beef mountain.

But the spark that has rekindled the optimism this morning is the breeding cattle which objectively has been such a poor success. We had two cows which were not so much autumn calvers as late or early spring calvers.

There was a Jersey which despite being 15 years old had still a complete udder and was given one more chance. She had taken it but was very late. And then there was the only remaining member of the Simmental herd of which I was once so proud. She calves every November and refuses to come forward even a week... and I'm far too mean to let her slip back four months to calve in the spring.

Anyway, with the dark nights and the disgusting weather, I decided to take the two in so that they might be observed in comfort at all hours.

I could have saved myself the bother. The Jersey calved a fine heifer calf last Sunday. I was there but she'd have managed just as well without me. The pure Simmental did not appear to be far on having a slack udder, a stiff tail and a tight rear end. I didn't even have a look when I came back from the discussion group on Sunday evening. But in the morning she had not one but two fine strong bull calves.

That was a brave sight for me but being on the slats they were not pretty. I wasn't going to hide these away. Soon I had a bale of straw down to the slatted shed and had them deep bedded. I know I will curse myself when they have to be mucked. But in the meantime I am enjoying dragging anyone who comes to call down to see the twins... and what is farming all about anyway... there is no use doing it for the money.

Beating an early retreat

DAMNABLE THOUGH it is, and much as I resent the slur on our great industry, I have accepted the inevitable and diversified. Little Ardo is now the home, not just of Ardo Pedigree Cattle but of the Ardo Publishing Company. And the proof of that was the launch on Saturday of the first volume of this *Farmer's Diary* along with the Turnbull cartoons.

The plan was to combine a reception in the Salmon Inn for the intellectuals of Aberdeen, the booksellers and the press, with the second annual Ladies Night of the Sunday Discussion Group. Mossie would get some of the sirlion roasts for which Aberdeenshire is famous, see that they were hung for three weeks and then barbeque them on his mobile converted rotaspreader. The Red Rooster would raid his tattie shed for some good bakers and the Salmon Inn would put up some nice salads and sweets.

And thus it was that a diverse company of some 70 souls gathered at the Salmon late on Saturday afternoon.

I soon realised I had a bit to learn about my new diversification. How for example do you 'launch' a book. Do you break a bottle of champagne over it and ask God to bless all that read in it? It was decided that we should have an unveiling ceremony. I swithered between an old velvet curtain which once hung in our sitting room and my daughter's scarlet gown from her student days at St Andrews.

I was a bit hurt when Fiona told me that that was all too pretentious. She insisted I cover the books with an old North Eastern feed bag in deference to all the times that had been used to entice cattle out of fields in the days before we got the three-wheeled dog called Honda.

There was no such problem about who would perform the unveiling. The Chairman of the Royal Highland and Agricultural Society, Jack Sleigh, is a neighbour and a reader of the

Glasgow Herald. Not only that but, just as the judge is supposed to buy his champion at the calf sales, Jack would likely feel bound to buy a book.

The Sleighs are a formidable family. Their mythology is considerable and well known and yet I was able to tell our guest of honour a story about his grandfather which he had not heard before.

Old John Sleigh was a renowned judge of horse and of men. At Ellon feeing market one year he had more or less struck a bargain when he thought he noticed that the man had something not quite right among his feet. Just before handing over the arles that would have sealed the bargain he said, "would ye mind rinnin yersel oot a thirty yards or so." Those were the days when men were men and masters were masters. There is no record of whether the man did run himself out for inspection or indeed whether he took the job.

Anyway Mr Sleigh did say that while he had performed many little public duties in his time it was a new experience for him to launch a book from under a feed bag.

I then thanked the guests for having come, especially the man who had come from London for coming so far. Then, to be fair, I thanked my neighbour Gowkie for coming, as he had come as far as he could reasonably be expected to come.

Then less than an hour late we had the beef barbequed in two 30lb roasts on the bone. One of the intellectuals asked the chef if the beef had come from one of my beasts.

"Michty no," said Mossie. "Look at the size o' that sirloin. Charlie's beasts never live lang enough to get to that size." That seemed to me to be unnecessarily unkind but I have to say that the beef was close to perfection. If the Meat and Livestock Commission is serious about promoting beef let them get Mossie to do tastings of the right stuff hung long enough and not overcooked. He could start with all the big caterers I have ever gone to. That kind of beef is a different product from the usual great slab of bright red stuff that was keeping the grass down earlier the same week.

By the time we had eaten, the gathering was becoming more of a staggering and the boys were becoming quite excited about this literary occasion. Somebody asked Mossie to sign the cartoon of him setting off on the third year of his three year rotation (winter bar-

ley – oil-seed rape – Bermuda). That was a good idea and soon the Guru of the Grain Barons was holding a signing session with a queue. The Red Rooster was signing the cartoon of him spotting that the clutch on my grain drier was on squint, and Big Hamish was signing the picture of him enjoying a cuppa from the teasmaid in his £27,000 digger. The Mains was impressed with the panache of Hamish's signature. 'Professional,' he said "Just like a doctor. It could be onything."

I have to report that the intellectuals beat a retreat after the food and they were quickly followed by the booksellers.

Even the journalists baled out when it became more and more obvious that the boys were going to be boys despite the presence of their wives. We had the old farming pursuit of pulling the swingle tree though there being very few horse about these days we had to use a brush. There was Cumberland wrestling and an odd bothy challenge... to lift a chair by the bottom of one leg. Our strongest man seemed to be the Rooster who modestly put his success down to the amount of hard work he did, though no one else could figure out which muscles would benefit from driving a car madly all over the country and bawling down a mobile phone.

The highlight of the evening had to be brought forward. You see Big Hamish has been slimming and when it comes to a heavy drinking session he fairly misses the six stone he has lost. It was feared that his balance was going so we had the vote of thanks at half-past seven. There was never such a vote of thanks. Standing like Colossus on the fireplace he thanked everybody he could think of and when he ran out of people to thank he thanked them all again... and again. And he brought the house down by finishing with; "And I would jist like to remind Charlie that withoot us he wad be naething."

He may have been exaggerating but it would certainly have been more difficult to write the book without the boys and less fun launching it.

December 16, 1991

Stuck at point of no return

I HAVE good news and bad news from the little farm on the hill. And, like the coward I have always been, I will start with the good.

The last of the pigs went to market and have yielded a profit. It isn't much but one has to pleased with any profit these days.

The 350 of them cost me just under £10,000. They then ate just over £10,000 worth of feed and converted it into meat at the rate of three pounds of feed to one pound of pork. They sold for a bit under £22,000. In all I was left with £1,706 and an ocean of muck for my time, effort and cash investment.

This modest surplus is 52 pence per pig better than I did with my previous two batches which were the property of the Grampian Country Group. They took all the risk and gave me £4.25 per pig.

It might have been a lot better. I had nine deaths this time as opposed to none when I was looking after Grampian's pigs. That would have contributed to the rise in the conversion rate from 2.82 to 3.00. And it seems like I paid far too much for the feed. There'll have to be a tough negotiation before the next batch goes in. We could have had another £4.00 a pig.

It is very good to have a stake in the profitable pig for that animal is quite unsubsidised by the Common Market. In fact if we were to go onto world prices for grain (the main input) we would be making much more money out of them.

When we were loading the last batch we came upon the sad sight of one 100 kilo pig in what appeared to be its death throes. Where you have livestock you do tend to get deadstock so we were brave about it... bunged him out into the sick pen and forgot about him. He took the death rate up to 2.5 per cent so there was nothing good about that.

But that wasn't the bad news. It was the bovines that provided that... and at six fif-

174

teen on Thursday morning. The phone rang. Gerry who lives in one of our cottar houses rang to say there were cows passing his bathroom window and had caused him to cut himself and he wasn't pleased.

I wasn't pleased either. The cows were heifers and they were headed for the main road. I jumped into the car and drove madly round the bumpy road which would get me to the main road before them. Half-way round the drive shaft of my car became discouraged by a particularly severe bump and I was stuck. I was, as near as I could guess it, at the exact point of no return. So I abandoned my car in the middle of the old road and set off at what would once have been a run.

Visions of huge articulated lorries ploughing into my heifers and into my bank balance spurred me to great efforts and seemed to subdue the arthritic pains from the old knees. When cars passed me I hid my stick and pretended that I had rediscovered my youth and gone back the early morning run.

I needn't have sweated for when I got to the cross roads there was no signs that my beasts had beaten me to it. In fact they had found an open gate to a grass park and were even happy to follow me home.

I had the Armstrong hired that day to give me peace to write a few words of my diary but that proved a middling investment. I was getting on tolerably well when 15 600 kilo steers passed the window. They were in high spirits and the mess they made of the garden beggars description. The only consolation was that Fiona, who leaves for her job in the toon before seven and doesn't get back till well after dark at this time of year, wouldn't see the damage till about April.

It was an odd thing, but the Armstrong had made a particular point of shutting the gate properly so it couldn't possibly have been his fault that they escaped. And yet there the gate was, open to the wide world.

You have to be a real jailer at this time of year to keep the cattle in when the food is scarce and we had the heifers out again that day. It was no wonder really. The Armstrong and Potions the chemist had put up a new bit of fence for them which was hung about as tightly as Christmas decorations... but they won't get out again.

I was very depressed about my farming after that day but I have to report that I am better pleased with it now. You see I have discovered that all is not plain sailing with my diversification either.

I always knew that, as a writer who would publish his own books, the biggest trouble would be marketing. How right I was.

You feel such a burke standing there in the Christmas shopping queue with your sample to show the manageress who has selling on her mind. When you reach the top of the queue you hold out the book apologetically to her and make a daft remark like "This frost will fairly keep the mildew aff the barley".

She scans the book impatiently and then with a smile that would freeze the diesel says, "How much is it?"

"£12.50" you say even more apologetically.

She puts the book in a paper bag and says, "That'll be £12.50, sir."

"No, no. You see that is my book," you stammer, lunging for the volume, at which point you find yourself trying to sell your book to the store detective...

Sound that stock man dreads

ON WEDNESDAY I shot out of bed. I usually delay and coorie doon for at least two five-minuters... not this time. For I had been awakened by the sound a stock farmer most dreads... cattle roaring. In the night that means a break-out.

As I hauled on the breeks I saw that it was four thirty. Any hopes I might have had that it was just some of them getting restless in anticipation of their morning feed could be set aside.

There had been another breakout to add to those heifers running off and the Armstrong definitely not leaving the stots' gate open so that they could go and replan the wife's flower garden and the croquet lawn.

As I rushed outside I was relieved to find that they had not yet made it to the garden or to the bags of barley that were sitting handily at the byre and the old barn, where the feeding stots were getting restive.

It must be the cows from the hill who would be down at the slatted shed making a mess of the beasts' silage and pillaging their barley.

As I ran down the close it seemed that the noise wasn't coming from the sheds. Indeed it seemed to be coming from the field in which the hill cows are fed their silage. But the noise was terrifying. The cows and the bull were bellowing for all they were worth. Something was not to their liking. I have only once seen cows like that before. That was in summer time. About a dozen of them milled round something in the grass bellowing and pawing the ground. It turned out to be a pheasant who for some reason froze there, terrified, instead of flying away. I have still no idea why the cows were so excited by it.

But this time it was quite dark and I couldn't see what was exciting them.

As I drew nearer I began to hear another noise through the roaring. It was a snuffling and grunting sound. I've never seen a badger hereabouts and I thought it might be one of those until I remembered the dying pig we'd found when we loaded the last of my fat porkers. He had clearly made a miraculous recovery and gone to discover the wider world.

It wasn't worth going back to bed but I went in for a very happy breakfast. Even though one pig is more of a nuisance than anything else it is encouraging when they live... it was a welcome Christmas bonus.

Apart from little excitements like that my farming is really a bit boring just now. I start at seven and I'm usually finished feeding at half-past eight. Cattle numbers are down a bit just now at 125 but they are in six different lots or they could be done much more quickly. One pig doesn't take much feeding and in fact, as it is all automatic, it doesn't take long to feed the 350 pigs when we are full.

So all I have to do is watch the crops grow and they're not doing much of that in this frosty weather. The spraying is all done until February and the manure is all on until spring temperatures force the plants into action. I could, of course, tidy-up and I sometimes do... a bit, and sometimes I worry about the loosebox roof, part of which blew off in 1987... but that's a job for summertime

surely.

It was all so much better fun when we had calves to rear and when we had pedigree cattle that could be washed and groomed and taken for walks. But that is surely young men's work. And where are the young men?

I was reading the other day that half the farms in Britain have no heirs waiting to take them on. That headline shocked many people but it didn't surprise me. I have two daughters who I call the Investments because they are good girls who worked hard at school and are far too valuable to walk bulls up and down the road or to feed calves. And I have two sons whom I call the Wasting Assets. Their ideas on expenditure could never be supported by a two hundred and fifty acre arable croft.

The Wasting Assets left school just before they properly could, lied about their ages and went to work on oilrigs for more money than their teachers had been getting.

Like oilmen they walk
Like Yankees they talk
There's no much in common
Tween my sons and me.

When we talk about work we are always at cross-purposes. When we talk about rates for a job I keep thinking they're talking days when they are only talking hours.

Indeed the Wasting Assets are not even happy with returns in the North Sea. One has come ashore to run night clubs in Tenerife in summer and London in winter and is always on the point of making a fortune... if the poor farmer would just lend him a couple of grand to tide him over.

The other has got fed up of the hardship of only having two weeks holiday out of four and has bought a restaurant so that he can be with his girlfiend all the time. That investment should be paid back in six years. There is not much scope for enticing that sort of chap onto the land and less chance that he could survive if you did.

So on this land
I've made me own
I struggle on alone.
But it's nearly over now
And now I'm easy."

Tears shed as tale unfolds

IT'S BEEN a difficult holiday. First the Breadwinner went down with the flu and then I quickly followed. I know there is nothing so boring as people telling you about their ailments or showing you their scars but my health has been so much more important to me than my farming that I must tell you something of it.

The good news was that I had the Armstrong hired from the machinery ring and the younger of the Wasting Assets was home. It was always going to be a joy to see him for Christmas as it was to be the first time for many years. Working over the holidays is the price he pays for being in the entertainment business and we understand that, but we don't have to like it. We always set a place for him just in case he turns up after all.

This year Jay's seat would be full and the turkey would have to be three pounds heavier. But, as it turned out, his return was a far greater boost than that... with the Wasting Asset around I was able to be really ill without worrying about the farm.

I was able to worry about being able to write anything for you, however. So when the fever was at its worst I forced myself to write down exactly how I felt. I thought hard about it and this is what I came up with:

It seemed to me that I had toothache on the lower half of my right jaw. I also had the same type of stouning centred just above and behind my eyes. Then behind my neck, the base of my spine, my bowel, my right thigh, knee and ankle, and my left ankle all had toothache as well. My eyeballs seemed to have become lined with something smoother than sandpaper but not as smooth as emery paper. Looking round was far less painful by moving the aching neck than by scratching the eyeballs.

But the thing that was most alarming was that the oxygen to sustain all that misery had to be

180

ingested though a nose that was lightly packed with dry cotton-wool, and bronchial tubes which were lined with more cotton wool which tickled as it threatened to become detached but never did.

I have coped with this crisis many times before using the theory developed by generations of my family, that there was nothing short of death that wouldn't succumb to half a pint of whisky, half a pint of boiling water, a spoonful of honey and half a dozen aspirins.

The theory was that the concoction gave you a prodigious, bed-drenching sweat which left you cold and the fever broken.

Three nights the cure produced nothing but nightmares.

Then when the cure was being prepared on the fourth night the Investment pointed out, what I had always known but had not understood, that I should not be mixing the antibiotics the doc had given me with folk-medicine. The whisky was cut down to a pub double, the sweat came on, the fever broke, and Christmas Day dawned delicate but at least possible.

Christmas Day was maybe not the best time for an ancestor-worshipping peasant to hear a family tale of a baby for whom there had appeared to be no room at the inn.

After the Wasting Asset, our guest of honour this year was my father's very much younger cousin Benjie and his exotic girl-friend Ursula. He is a gentle thoughtful man who is always welcome partly because he reminds me of the man who looked after this hill before me. His mother and my father's mother were sisters and friends.

When my father was conceived, out of wedlock, his father, like so many in that time, quickly emigrated to California. His jilted love quickly followed on the boat, though to Canada, in which place she met and married a man called Willows with whom she had three children and lived a full life for the rest of her days.

That left my father to be brought up by his grandparents. It was the childhood, so full of love and of wonder, that he described in his book *Farmer's Boy*. There were bits passed over in the book which were not so wonderful. Like taking to school the birth certificate with 'illegitimate' scrawled over it, and the constant tormenting from his Uncle Charles.

All that we knew. But on Christmas Day Benjie brought with him documents which threw a new perspective on this most sensitive part of our family history. I was able to produce the birth certificate which showed that John Robertson Allan had been born to Eliza

Jane Allan, not in his grandparents' Parish of Whitestripes, but at Udny where Eliza Jane was a 'domestic servant'.

The lassie, it seems, had decided to leave her shame behind and head for Canada and had made some sort of arrangement for her son. We think the old folks may not have known of the baby. It would have been quite possible for a big girl to conceal it from her parents when domestic servants were fee-ed for six months at a time. At any rate they had found out, claimed their grandson and proceeded to give him the childhood immortalised in *Farmer's Boy*.

One of Benjie's documents was a letter written in 1981 by the grandson to his aunt. *I remember darkening winter afternoons when you were stirring the porridge on the kitchen fire and I sat beside you hoping for the sweetie I always got. Then I realised how very lucky I was – a bastard put away somewhere and then saved by my grandparents who made me their own. I feel great gratitude even now after 75 years. No bairn could have had a gentler, more loving, time. One thing was the way you protected me from Chae. He wasn't really bad to me but he did torment me*

182

in a hard way. I guess now he was a bit jealous and resented the old people and you being so kind. It was all very wonderful and I remember it so clearly. In the last few years my memory has been failing. I forget names I forget people. I forget facts — even the sort out of which I made a good living for many years, and that seems very strange for I made most of those facts up myself. But you, I am sure, I'll never forget, till the end of the last day."

My eyes filled, the cotton-wool melted and I almost drowned.

Mossie gets his sums all wrong

WELL THAT'S it official. The beef job just can't be made to pay. Mossie has tried it and made a loss so what more proof does the government want?

I told you that the farmer of Mossside had decided to change his farming philosophy. Despite having an enviable reputation as a pig-man, despite the fact that grain growers crowd round him in bars in the hope that he may let slip the secret of the five tonne wheat crop, despite the fact that spies from the Scottish Agricultural College are after the cocktail of chemicals with which he grows his rape crops, Mossie has gone over to subsidy farming.

I am delighted to say that the new European arrangements are all in favour of the inefficient like me and against the high output characters like Mossie... and quite right too. If there is a problem of too much output it is certainly not me that is causing that. And this is to be recognised in the new rape regime. Now we are to get most of our support just for sowing the rape and never mind how small a crop we get. An extra kilo of crop will be worth half as much as last year so Mossie's going to use much less chemical, much less fertiliser and lose much less sleep about his crops.

Indeed, he's going to grow linseed in the hope he can be like that chap last year who grew £19 worth of linseed and got a planting grant of £240. Yes, Mossie has become a subsidy junky and that's how, despite the fact that he is used to pouring scorn on those who would waste their time with cattle, he came to have 90 stots last back-end.

His approach was typical. Off to Orkney. Buy the best forward stores. Nothing but the best and no more than 90 as that is all you get the subsidy on. Keep them eight weeks and no more because that is how long you need to keep them to qualify for the Beef Special Premium. Keep them all together in a court made of big square bales in his grain store. Feed them a complete and delicious ration made up to maximise growth by the finest brains in the agricultural supply trade out of a specially smiddy-made hopper. Two scoops with the digger per day and the whole £60,000 worth were fed.

When I looked at my 50 feeding cattle in five lots spilling their barley I had fed them out of laboriously bagged bruising amongst the bree from their silage soup, I found the prospect of Mossie the beefman deeply depressing.

I'm feeling better now, though.

The cattle left Mossside the week before Christmas at a damned good fixed price because he had so many good even cattle. But then Mossie started to make mistakes. He started to calculate how much profit he had made in his eight weeks.

Including the subsidy he had raised the stots an average of £115, which was clearly acceptable, not to say extremely good. But he should have stopped his calculating there. The feed-mix had cost £75 a head, silage cost £8, the money tied up was worth £12, killing charges were £16, and transport was £5. It was a grand loss

of £1 per head... not counting his labour, but then, who counts that these days?

Any experienced cattleman could tell Mossie that he had achieved a pretty satisfactory result and far above average, but he is disappointed. He reflects sadly that he could have had a profit if only the one that died had lived. That would have raised the selling average by seven pounds a head.

It is all a bit pathetic, like the crofter on Skye who boasted that if only he'd lost another couple of ewes he could have had a lambing percentage of 100.

Subsidies or no subsidies Mossie should leave the beef job to those who understand it.

You see I had stots away at the same time as Mossie and I was quite happy with my returns. Of course I didn't get as much as I was expecting but then I never expect to get as much as that. And I certainly didn't spoil the thing by going and counting the cost of barley at the going rate of £120 a tonne. If it is counted at all, it will be at the value (less drying charges) at which it entered the grain tower at harvest time.

And you can't go counting the cost of borrowed money. No man on earth can make cat-

tle pay on borrowed money. No, no the correct rate of interest to charge the enterprise is zero. Otherwise you can't keep cattle and cattlemen must, by definition, keep cattle.

I assessed my stots' performance like this. They cost £490 in April. They ran about all summer on the grass I had anyway and needed £3 worth of wormer when they came in. Since then they have eaten silage which we made ourselves and ate barley at a fair rate. But that all came out of the tower and as there is still plenty coming out there must still be some left so that can't have been a big expense.

The cheque from the mart came to £630 a head and there's the subsidy of £32 to come so, whereas Mossie made a loss on his stots I have a profit on mine of a good £100 a head.

Wonderful isn't it? And next year it will be wonderful again.

Crookie casts eyes eastwards

WHEN WE start to hang the capitalists they'll fall over themselves to sell us the rope.

Joe Stalin said that, when he was laying the foundations of the desert that was once the Soviet Union.

For nearly all my adult life it seemed extremely likely that the Russians and their allies would soon be hanging most of us capitalists, for they were always making another pretty impressive start on the job... as they did in Cuba.

The picture of the capitalist, himself in the queue for the gallows, selling the hangman a new rope seemed to me to be depressing but altogether credible.

Luckily the Soviets could not even afford to buy the rope now. And yet we are still queueing up to make a sale.

Not of rope, mind you, but of our agricultural technology. Our pig breeders are falling over themselves to sell them their seed-stock, our food-processing companies are over in Moscow advising on what the Russians are doing to spoil the food after it leaves the farms, and the Steppes and the Caucuses are in danger of being over-run by a plague of agronomists in green wellies.

I told you that the Red Rooster was over in Germany looking at land. He decided that he had enough problems at home but now another of the discussion group is looking East... he likes what he sees.

Crookie is our potato King and he's been eyeing the Russian market. He sums up the predicament of the Russians like this. "They hinna got good tatties. They canna grow them. They canna lift them. They've nae richt storage for them, nae distribution system, nae richt packaging and nae idea where to start."

Crookie's in a group that are going to give the Russians a start. They've been over to the Ukraine and been impressed. They have seen the fine flat fields that stretch for miles.

They've seen the rich loam that is 10 feet deep without a stone in it. And they've also seen what an economic shambles can be like.

I've seen one too... in Zambia where it was brought into particular focus in our four star hotel. At breakfast there was only cornflakes. No bread, butter and marmalade or coffee like the brochure said. Just cornflakes with water... there was no milk either.

But Crookie's pals would have found our Zambian Hotel a treat. Their hotel couldn't offer them anything for breakfast at all. In fact it's becoming clear that, with the exceptions of the space programme and the armed forces, the Former Soviet Union, far from being a super power is a third world area and pretty far down the development league at that.

At least their potato job will soon be on the mend. The boys are going to send over the best of Scottish seed. But they're not going to let a third world shambles destroy that seed. They're going to go with the cargo to ensure that it isn't frosted or diverted to the black market and eaten. They're going to plant the potatoes themselves with their own equipment. They're going to see the whole job through to marketing. It will teach the Russians a lot if they have a mind to learn.

The boys are hoping to learn a thing or two as well. They've already been warned that the Scots lads who go out to drive their machinery should only be sent for a fortnight at a time. The first week they draw gasps of amazement from the former Soviets as they get their heads down and tear on with the work. The second week they star again but by this time the head is up and they adopt the anxious look of the stag on the hill. The third week they are off with the chairman of the local co-op's daughter.

On the other hand, our potato Barons discovered that when it comes to strong drink their Russian hosts were absolutely peerless. Bottle after bottle of vodka slipped down with no apparent effects on the Russians but devastating the visitors from Scotland. Of course it is no wonder they can hold their liquor. They get so much practice and there is so little else in the shops.

The authorities have a startling policy on strong drink. Until the recent reforms vodka was sold at about one tenth of the cost of production. That meant that a bottle was costing in the region of tuppence. With nothing else in the hotel for breakfast you would soon acquire a head for the stuff.

Of course the lads couldn't believe it was as simple as that and vowed that they would set a trap for the Russians when they visited Scotland. They set their guests up with a rare treat of some 100 proof malt whisky and settled back to sip gently at the blends and watch the Russians go legless.

They were sorely disappointed. The quests gobbled up the malt (at a cost equivalent to 1,000 bottles of their own vodka each) with no apparent effect. They were soon helping out with the blends. They were as bright as buttons at breakfast the next day while their hosts didn't dare to shake their heads in disbelief.

I must confess to envying Crookie and his pals. This deal is going to be a great experience. But I wonder if old Joe Stalin will be looking up and saying "I told you so".

Not quite Joe. It is even better than you predicted. The Russians have no real money to pay for all this help. The capitalist governments are going to have to pay for the rope.

Januaery 20, 1992

The stench brings us together

I AM not very popular with the housewives of the district. I have been mucking out the piggery and spreading the muck on the stubble. Unfortunately that lies to the windward side of the two cottages which in happier times contained farm servants but are now let out.

In the old days, when everybody on the farm worked on the farm, there was no trouble with smells. When the fields were coated in pungent pig manure so were the menfolk, so the wives got used to it. But now that the men work off the farm at inorganic jobs and their womenfolk go out to work in offices you can understand their being a bit more sensitive.

Anyway I think the stink is a good thing. It brings those of us who work on the farm and those who live on the farm closer together. It reminds everyone that the farm is a place for producing food rather than

some sort of country park.

Mind you, the mucking is a poor affair these days. It only took us two days. Potions, the local chemist who comes to play even when it's pig manure, manned the muckspreader and tore up and down the road to the field spilling as much as he could, which made a fine pungent gour all along the road. I manned the old digger and the graip.

What a change. Whereas now I only need the graip for the difficult corners, in the 40s and 50s the mucking started and finished with the graip.

We had 80 tonnes of dry matter in the piggery but it was very far from dry so it must have been easily 200 tonnes of muck.

In the old days that would have taken the five of us a fortnight of toil. Two tractormen would have helped the grieve to load their carts graip by painful graipful. They would then have taken it out to the field where the orraman would have pulled the muck off in regular heaps using a thing we called a cleeck... a sort of long graip with toes bent at right angles.

My job was the worst. I had to spread the muck, by graip all on my own... all day. It was called 'breaking' the muck be-cause you had to try to break up the clumps and cover the field with an even fertile film. There was no hope of keeping anything like up, nor of slacking, as the grieve could see at a glance just how little you had done.

But it was easy this week. The digger tore the muck out half a tonne at a time and Potions plastered the field with a cascade of finely broken muck from the rotaspreader. No-one broke sweat.

Now we are ready for the next batch of pigs to arrive and the farm has settled down to resume its winter sleep. Where once there would have been five men hard at it all winter, now there is only work for me for about half the time.

I was pleased to get the last of the muck out but I have to admit to being rather sad to see the back of the last pig. You will recall that when we were putting the last batch away we found him lying apparently twitching his last. We thought no more about him until he caused uproar in the middle of the night by venturing forth among the cows.

Since then he has become something of a pet and a reminder of the days when every farmer's wife kept a pig to eat up the household scraps and produce a bit of nice cured pork for the winter. When I stayed with my grandmother during the war I was so hungry and so unfussy about whose plate my food came off that she used to say "There's nae use for a pig when you've Charles".

But we've plenty of use for a pig and he was offered all sorts of kitchen offal. He was most appreciative. Having been brought up on nothing but dry pig pellets he revelled in the mixed and even balanced diet he was offered. He ate everything, of course, but this pig was something of a vegetarian. He liked the outside leaves of cabbage and even lettuce and went quite wild when given half a dozen tangerines which the Breadwinner had over-ordered for the holiday season and which had gone off.

I can't say that the bonus piggie thrived though. I think that was mostly the cold. When there were 350 pigs in the shed it was cosy but the bonus was all alone and the shed was like an igloo. He responded by growing hair, so that, with the squint setting of his head, a legacy of his illness, he was not a bonny sight when we loaded him for market.

Still we miss him.

He went straight to the kill-ing house to which I am contracted and my cheque will be whatever they give me.

A dozen years ago, when I sold my last 70 outside sows, it was a different and far more sociable occasion. They went to Kittybrewster Mart and that let everybody have a go at my old dears.

Not that there was any great rush. In fact the only bidder seemed to be a most charismatic bandit called Edward Johnstone. Now one bidder should be enough if the auctioneer knows his job, but I was displeased with the first sale or two so I started bidding. When the bandit realised where the opposition was coming from he protested loudly to the auctioneer. He seemed to think that I should only be allowed to bid once.

The auctioneer and I disagreed and I continued to bid away until I was satisfied. And I couldn't have bid too much as Edward bought the lot.

Surprised that I didn't disappear immediately the bandit came round to ask if I had more pigs to come. I had to admit that I had stuck my knee in the railings and couldn't move

He's been dining out on that one for years... "better than any luck-penny," he said.

"No Sir, we don't do sales"

THE BREADWINNER has been hinting for some time that she would appreciate an eternity ring. But I'm afraid that, though I am normally a most sensitive person, I didn't pick up the hints. When Christmas came and I only produced William Boyd's latest novel (which she'd already bought for herself anyway) she stopped the hints and came right out and asked for a ring.

I am even more afraid that I still didn't take the thing seriously enough. Well, I couldn't see that there was anything wrong with the previous one. And maybe it was her attitude to that that spoiled Fiona's case. She had been very patient about a proper engagement ring and had been thrilled to bits when I turned up to see our fourth-born bearing her solitaire diamond ring.

The news flashed round the hospital and the nurses were soon flocking round "the lady in ward seven who's just got engaged".

Indeed I might have been getting away with it even now had it not been for Crookie. You see our potato farmer and grain baron is in love, or something very like it. That is not a condition with which our man is very familiar and we are all impressed. So is he. So much so that in the run up to Christmas he found himself in one of the more expensive jewellers in Aberdeen.

He was impressed there too. He told me about this simple gold necklace with some shiny bits on it which cost over £600. Stupidly I told the Breadwinner about this and that really did it. "And how long has he known her? Two months and she gets a £600 necklace. And I've put up with you for 32 years which seems like 62 years and I get a paperback?"

In no time it was round all the wives and the boys were all heading for town. My immediate inclination was Ratner's because they had a sale on but that wouldn't do. Mossie had

193

Aye, noo. Whit's the right price o' this?

already done his shopping and advised me to go to an old established jewellers in Aberdeen. "They're nae the worst and they've a sale on." When he'd been coming out of that shop he'd bumped into Sandy Fowlie (my cattle buyer). Mossie had got discount of course but not poor Sandy.

It's funny how our wives are so ashamed of us when we ask for discount. How else are we to cope with the current economic climate? And just because you get a luck-penny on your ring doesn't mean it looks any cheaper. And you can always tell your friends it cost the full price (or even more).

Anyway when she'd got

him cornered and they were driving into town Mrs. Fowlie had read a riot act which went something like this… "and you shall not ask for discount… and you shall not say 'how much for a quick deal'… and you shall not say 'how much do I get off if I pay cash?' I'll choose, you'll pay and keep shtumm."

You see Val had just heard of the ordeal of her friend Suzanne. She had been shopping with her husband Edward the Bandit, the pig buyer I was telling you about last week. They had decided to settle for a set of crystal glasses and a decanter when Edward asked the posh assistant "Aye, noo. What's the right price of this?"

"I don't understand you sir. The price is written on the decanter."

Suzanne understood her husband only too well and started to take an interest in a tray of brooches at the other side of the shop. She hid her blushes further into the tray when she heard Edward say "Aye aye. I see the price ticket but what's the *right* price? I mean you canna possibly want £118 for a joog and puckle glesses."

When the assistant still claimed to be bemused Edward asked to see her superior.

By this time Suzanne was out of the shop and by the time he was asking the superior for the 'right price' she was back in the car muttering about never taking her husband shopping again. It's a funny thing about wives but she wasn't even placated when Edward came back with the decanter and glasses. The right price had apparently been the round £100.

Luckily I didn't take the Breadwinner when I went for her eternity ring, and I was quick to make the point that I wasn't going to be an easy touch. While pretending to study the tray of dear rings and the tray of very dear rings the assistant brought me, I told him "You know I came here because I was told you were the least unreasonable of the dear shops and also because you had a sale on. I'm a bit worried now as I see no sign of a sale."

"No sir we don't have sales. Why should we? We don't sell fashion jewellery. All our pieces are classic designs and we know we'll sell them eventually. What we will do (at any time of year) is give small discount to a client who comes and buys something nice from us."

"And what do you call a small discount?"

"Oh... ten per cent."

"Well, at least we've got a start," said I.

I bought a pretty six-diamond ring and screwed the discount up to approximately 13.72 per cent.

The Breadwinner was delighted. And so, in truth, was I. But we were all a bit sore on Sunday night when it emerged that Crookie, who had started it all, had only been looking at jewellery. He hasn't bought anything at all... yet.

Breadwinner gives order for tidy-up

BIG HAMISH is in trouble with the wife. You see the Big Man was telling us at the discussion group that meets in the Salmon Inn on Sunday evenings, about the change that has come over the countryside in the recent, difficult years.

"Every one of my neighbours' wife gins oot tae work," he told us. Now, Hamish has three farms and he must have 30 neighbours in all so it's unlikely to be exactly true but there is an awful lot of it about. We all shook our heads and agreed that it was a sad thing that our male chauvinism had been so beaten down by our circumstances.

But it wasn't any of that that got Hamish into trouble. You see he not only said "Aye, my wife's the only one that hasn'a got a job," but someone told Heather.

Now I have some sympathy with the lass for even feeding Hamish is quite a contract... especially since he went on the high fibre, low fat diet. In the old days he used to stop in by the bakers for a few pies on his way home to his dinner. Those took the rough edge off his appetite. But now the not-quite-so-big man arrives home ravenous and needs a mountain of salad and coleslaw to see him through the afternoon.

She also has two children to put out and the house to keep, of course, but any housekeeper has that. What made Heather mad was that she is also 'the office' for Hamish's three farms and his contracting business as well as being relief baillie for his dairy herd.

Of course everybody except Heather knew what the Big Man meant but we do wish he would be a bit more tactful. None of us whose wives go out to work can afford to offend them and far less can Hamish.

Certainly I go to great lengths to appease my own Breadwinner. She goes off to town before seven to play with computers and doesn't get home till after six. In theory she

196

gets the benefits of living in the country on a lovely old farm. So it is and so she does, but you see the Breadwinner is a banker's daughter and she must have everything tidy. She does not find it adds to her standard of living that instead of living in suburbia she has to drive past heaps of plastic bags and rusting machinery, not to mention the tumbledown fences and the guttering falling off the steading, to alight in a close inches deep in that gourie mud that is three parts muck.

The Breadwinner went away to work happy this morning for I have spent the weekend redding up the farm.

I discovered a few weeks ago that the nearest thing to an easy way to tidy a farm was to get a skip from the council and tip everything into it. One of their lorry drivers told me about the 'service' and he also told me that, as part of the council's attempts to keep the district tidy, I would get a skip for nothing. It actually cost £28 but by that time it was ordered.

Into that skip went at least a year's plastic bags. It was enough to convince me that we should get rid of the rest. But when I phoned the council their free service had risen to £58 and that was just not on. I know you are wondering why I didn't just buy a box of matches. The answer is that unless you burn it in a special oven of the type Rechem said they had at

START REDDING UP, NOW!!

Bonnybridge you will release dioxins ("the most deadly chemical known to man") and we've enough troubles without that.

Anyway the discussion group saved the day. It turns out that Big Hamish has a skip. It is an old 17 tonne lorry adapted for the tractor and he has a quarry to dump the contents.

It arrived on Saturday morning and I yoked the digger at ten. It was just high enough to reach the skip and in went the plastic. The second target was the two cart loads of tyres I had fetched from a dump to keep down the covers of the pits in the days before we baled the silage.

Then we tackled the dump where for 20 years we have thrown discarded machinery, paling posts, netting wire and buckets with holes in them. That is right in the close so we can never be tidy as long as that is the dump. The digger dug and dumped and I was ruthless. I even let two old iron shafts which would once have pulled a horse-drawn Bone-Davie go. I felt bad about that but not about the expensive mixer that never successfully mixed the feed for the barley beef bulls that I used to pour good money after.

I was unable to throw away the old granite roller we found in the dump nor the old stone strainer. They've been retained to make features round our ever-so-tidy farm. As I write, the great skip is full... I have pounded it with the digger but she will take no more. She is a brave sight for perched right on top are the two old cars which we have been using to scare the doos off the rape... we can't have scrap about the place any longer.

The former dump is to go down to grass... Potions has a ride-on mower which he brings down to play, and we've taken a half share in Big Hamish's motorised close brush.

It's all nonsense of course. You would think I had forgotten the sage's advice that "Ye canna tak the rent oot o' the close". But the balance of power on the farm nowadays is such that when the Breadwinner says 'action' and looks like she means it, action it has to be.

Pigeons get benefit of doubt

IT IS well over 40 years since that bleak day in March when I persuaded my mother that the excitement of spring was so close that we should go for a nature walk. Weeks of snow had given way to rain and mud though there was still a collar of snow round the dykesides. The prevailing colour of the fields was brown, the dark brown of the fields awaiting the seeds (for there was no winter crop then) and the lighter tired brown of the grass as it waited for the first warm breath and the first sprinkling of nitrogen.

We wrapped up well in our matching furry coats and set forth into that unpromising environment in search of the first harbingers of the renewal that

spring always brought.

What the young naturalist expected to find I cannot really remember, but the walk was a sad disappointment. In the garden we found that the snowdrops were out, that the crocuses were well on and the daffodils were trying hard. The flowering currant that my father had planted as a first step to civilising the wild and bare farm he'd returned to after the war was well in bud. But when it came to wild nature it was a blue do.

After hunting the sides of the road and the banks of the little stream that wound down the brae to the village we sat down on the Postie's Seat... a wild knap sometimes called the Broom Hillie after its principal vegetation. The broom provided shelter and it was not as cold as it might have been, but I had to admit we were a bit early for spring.

"I doot there's nae much nature aboot the day," I said sadly, and a crow, which certainly didn't count as nature, cawed in bleak concord with the thin wind.

What a contrast today. Here we are, hardly into February, and nature is hard at it. There hasn't been any snow that has been cold enough to cover the ground. Fields are green with winter crops that are offering to grow. The wheat is trying so hard it is showing signs of stress through lack of nitrogen.

And the grass has grown a little all winter. We still have 30 bulling heifers outside. They get a bale of silage soup every second day and for the rest they eat grass. That's not what you would call luxuriating but there is always a fresh green shoot for the 30 mouths. I'll have to take them in this week though because, with the weather being so mild, the ground is beginning to poach and we'll need the grass in summertime.

I suppose it has a lot to do with the trees with which my farther crowned the little hill that looks across the Ythan valley, but there is always plenty of nature about now. The winter cereals and rape, which provide a green bite all winter, will have helped too. We have pheasants and partridges everywhere, and a fox to dine thereon. He lives in a row of bales. The flowering currant which now surrounds the old farmhouse is springing into leaf and the crocuses are coming. We have at least two sparrow hawks neither of which would be here if it wasn't for the flocks of pigeons that are flying to the oil-seed rape.

Now, in previous winters, myself and Willie the Hunter have waged what we call the Pigeon Wars against the blue hoard that can strip a field of rape to the roots. And I've told you about the strategic disagreement between myself as commander in chief and Willie the Hunter my 2.I.C... Willie would happily watch the blue termites undermining the foundations of my wealth as they grazed over the field into range of his gun. That way he killed quite a number. But I had no interest in murder. All I wanted was to scare the damned things onto my neighbours' crops.

The troops would be waiting patiently until they could see the yellows of the pigeon's eyes when round the corner would come that damned fool officer and start jumping up and down and shooting into the air. Those were bad moments.

They are all over now though. The tension between the cushets and me has gone as quickly as that between the Kremlin and the Pentagon. It was always debatable whether the cushets did more harm than good because it never seemed to matter how bad the devastation in the winter, the rape always seemed to recover. Still, with an extra cwt of crop worth £12 we thought it well worth waging war, even on suspicion.

All has changed. Because of a change in the way the market is organised it is just not worth bothering. The EEC are to give us £150 or so an acre just to grow the rape and they are halving the price. That means we will only get an extra £6 for each extra cwt of seeds. At that level we'll give the pigeons the benefit of the doubt.

And we're cutting down on other inputs too. Because the extra bit of output is worth so much less we are cutting down our fertilisers by about a quarter and our chemical sprays by half. This will, I hope, make the new regime good for my balance sheet which has much need. But it is very bad news for the grain trade. There is just bound to be less for them to sell. And it is very bad news indeed for the agro-chemical industry.

But if all be true, they tell me now, and if all be true I hear, (that chemicals and fertilisers are polluting our environment) that will be very good news for the wildlife.

Next February Little Ardo will be fair hodging with nature.

Stumbling bull a snitch at 1500gns

I've been back to the Perth Bull Sales. Old Johnder was coming over his own stock and in truth he was pretty lucky to have come over their mothers in the first place for he was an average bull long ago when the average was not as high as it is today.

Tony O'Reilly the great Irish wing three-quarter and now the top man with Heinze (with an income said to be $75m a year) is credited with the remark that 80 per cent of Irishmen were, contrary to popular rumour, above average intelligence. When pressed about this remarkable statistic our man substantiated it by explaining that 80 per cent of Irishmen were above the average of the other 20 per cent.

Well, old Johnder was a bit like that and we must have new and better blood.

So it was off to Perth to buy a bull.

And once again I had it rubbed-in how the long squeeze on farm incomes has reduced the circumstances of the farmer of Little Ardo.

Ten years ago I would have sent my cattleman off to Perth on the Friday with the bulls we had to sell. I would have swanned down on the Sunday just in time for the Aberdeen Angus Society's Ceilidh. I'd have watched the judging of the Blacks and the Shorthorns on the Monday and then gone to the Shorthorn Dinner in the evening. That was a splendid do that with dancing of a particularly jolly kind.

Then on the Tuesday the Shorties and the Blacks were sold and we had the judging of our breed, the Simmentals. In the evening there was the Simmental Club's Annual Meeting followed by another dinner and more dancing. On the Wednesday, we got the bulls sold and away up the road with a pocketful of tin, to sort out which of the creditors to pay off.

Much of that conviviality still goes on, I'm told, but with no one to leave behind to do the work, socially this week's sales were a blue do for me.

I bolted out of bed on the Wednesday morning as soon as The Breadwinner's alarm went at the back of six. I ran round the beasts giving them their barley. Luckily there was nothing that I couldn't ignore though I did notice that one of my Black Hereford heifers didn't come to see me and I knew she would be outside somewhere calving. I'd never have found her in forty acres without a torch so it was back into the house, a cat's lick at the sink, changed and on the road to Perth by seven.

I was at the new Mart at Perth in time to have 25 minutes looking at Bulls before the start of the sale. Well, that was a hopeless contract with meeting so many of those with whom one drank so much too much on all those earlier and jollier sales. Everyone is older now but that doesn't mean they don't want to talk, like the old firm of Hogg and Todd from the Borders. Dave and Jim (it took me years to learn which was which – they were so inseparable that it seemed to make little difference) were the men who claimed immortality by taking a Simmental bull into one of the best hotels in town to gatecrash the Aberdeen Angus dinner which was a rather snooty affair at the time. There is still a glint in the four eyes but the four knees are starting, like mine, to show the benefits of too long spent chasing rugby balls.

And there were old pals who would not leave a man to find the best bull for his farm but would insist on showing him a bull that he wanted to sell. Robin Forrest from Duns insisted on showing me a bull which was so clearly out of my class that I was able to study one in a neighbouring pen which might suit my pocket.

He was called Durren Argus. He had a great 400 day weight despite having been bred in Caithness. He was also dark in colour and for some reason the market will always let you have a dark Simmental bull a bit cheaper. He was very fleshy (that is code for fat and suggests easy finishing which is essential on a poor place like this) and a good long bull but a bit plain about the head which would put off those who, above all, wanted something pretty to show the neighbours when they got home.

I watched 29 bulls, only four of which were bigger than Argus, pass through the ring at between 950 and 5,500 guineas. I had the occasional wave for practice but always at prices well below the danger level. It is worth doing that so that the auctioneer knows you are there and doesn't miss you when it comes to the main event.

When the great beast's turn came the doubts set in. He was indeed plain and dark but I got in and started waving. Then I had a stroke of luck, at least it will have been luck if my bull doesn't go off his legs. The bidding was at 1,500 and I was in when Argus seemed to hit a bump in the road, stumbled and almost fell.

Mobility is very important for bulls. If they can't chase the cows up to the top of the hill there is little hope of them doing much when they get there. So falling over, on flat ground, is the worst possible publicity for a bull. Bidding stopped immediately and I had a bull.

There would have been time for more than one pint with Jimmy Todd but times have changed so much that he didn't want a second. I was home by three o'clock to give the beasts the silage they should have had in the morning.

And the heifer I had no time for in the morning? She had managed quite well without me and was nursing a fine Belgian Blue heifer calf.

February 24, 1992

Not a dry eye in the house

My scheme for keeping this diary is to get up early and have it written before dawn cracks. That way the writing doesn't get in the way of the farming. It works well in the dead of winter but it becomes more and more difficult as the days grow longer and the nights shrink. And I can tell you that spring is on the way. Even now I can see the first chink of dawn so I must hurry for there is much to tell.

Sod's Law has been at it again. With the quite extraordinarily mild winter we have been enjoying, Mossie, who has become my honorary crops consultant, ordered the nitrogen to be put on the rape and the winter cereals on the tenth of February... a good three weeks ahead of our normal. No sooner was the stuff on than the skies darkened and we were hit by the first snow of winter.

I took this up with the honorary consultant and told him that he should have been more prudent. My fertiliser would surely be off down the hill to the River Ythan or away through the hole in the ozone layer before enough heat returned to Aberdeenshire to let it get to work on the crops. But my man tells me I am all right. The manure is not the simple jumping nuts we usually use but urea, and apparently urea doesn't leech. As soon as the snow is away I am assured of growth like I have never seen before.

But the main points of interest have not been farming as such. First there was the great football match between Huntly which rose from its usual position near the foot of the Highland League to challenge the might of Airdrie from the Premier League. We were very untypical football fans for this untypical match. After a very jolly lunch of smoked salmon, quails eggs and champagne we walked along to the little ground joking about how many we would lose by. In the event our Saturday afternoon footballers equalised with five minutes to go and we almost burst

205

ourselves with excitement. Thankfully we were saved a midweek trip to Airdrie by two further goals for the professionals.

It had been a great occasion for the little market town.

But then on Sunday we had and even more momentous day... the 80th birthday party given by his family for a man who 64 years ago was orraman here at Little Ardo. Maitland Mackie was no ordinary orraman of course. He was the boss's son who was serving his apprenticeship at his father's outfarm.

Now, on a stockfarm in Aberdeenshire in those days, an orraman's life in winter was depressingly predictable... he had to take his tapner to the field every day at six o'clock and top and tail turnips more or less all day, everyday.

The nearest thing to relief was that at about nine o'clock the cattleman, having finished sorting the beasts, would come out and join the orraman at the pu'in. Unfortunately that was not as great a boon as you might think, for the cattlemen was a surly sort of chap with a limited appetite for conversation. But the orraman tried hard.

"By God, Geordie," he had said one particularly frosty morning, "The neeps are caul this mornin."

"Well, dinna haud them sae lang." came the sour reply. The orraman still likes to tell that story against himself, but mainly, I think, so that he can explain what an unfair remark it was as he was easily keeping up with the cattleman and so could not have been holding the neeps any longer than him.

The orraman only had one winter at it and maybe the anticipation of that, was what was bugging the cattleman, but then it was off to the university and a BSc. His next job was grieve at another of his father's outfarms and, by the time he was 22, Maitland Mackie was into Westertown of Rothienorman where his son and namesake now has the biggest farming business in the North.

Our old orraman was an innovator in farming. He had the first combined harvester in the county, the first hen battery, the first deliveries of bottled milk and for many years the biggest overdraft. He became Dr. Mackie, Sir Maitland Mackie and Lord Lieutenant of the county without appearing to break sweat or to handle another neep.

There is a tradition of emigration in our family. As I look out of my window here I can see the spot where my great grandmother watched, without a tear in her eye, as the last of her three sons set off for the Empire never to return. And though he is luckier than that old lady, old Maitland Mackie suffers from emigration as his favourite of six is in Australia. At the great 80th birthday celebrations he proudly showed off a letter and a photograph that had arrived that morning from his darling Ruth.

Then it was time for the family's present. A huge box was brought in. Lady Mackie shuddered. She too has had 80 years to collect gear. Where on earth, let alone in their bungalow were they going to find room for such a bulky present.

"How nice of you to buy me a coffin," said the old man.

"Open the box. Open the box," we all cried.

The old man strode forward and opened his present. It was his missing daughter all the way from Australia. The six children were together for the celebration.

I don't really like the "This is Your Life" approach to emotion and when I am 80 I want to know who's coming so that I can order my nerves to deal with them all. But as the old man and the daughter who is no longer young, hugged and hugged one another, she still standing in the coffin, he, plastic hips not withstanding, trying to get in beside her, it was a most moving occasion.

There wasn't a dry eye in the house, or if there was, it certainly wasn't one of mine.